I0552736

Discerning readers checkout our catalog online at
www.shipwrecktbooks.press, or Google our titles.

Lost Lake Folk Opera

N7 Summer 2022 v1

FEATURING WRITERS
FROM THE LITERARY RENAISSANCE
TAKING PLACE IN NORTHFIELD, MINNESOTA

This Issue
ILLiberal Democracy

WWW.SHIPWRECKTBOOKS.PRESS

Shipwreckt Books no longer accepts paper submissions. Use the submissions portal at www.shipwreckt.press.

Cover art, interior design, and photography by Shipwreckt Books.
Page 76 image provided by John Torgrimson.
Page 88 from Northfield Poet Laureate website.

Shipwreckt Books Publishing Company LLC
Lost Lake Folk Opera magazine
153 Franklin Street
Winona, Minnesota, 55987

We acquire First North American Serial Rights (FNASR) upon acceptance and retain exclusive rights to your submission for six months following publication. Your piece will be archived and may be included in future retrospective editions. If you republish your work, please attribute first publication to *Lost Lake Folk Opera* magazine (Volume and Number).

Contents

Tom Driscoll, Managing editor

A Quick Note

olk Opera last dropped a new issue two years ago in late summer, the Special Covid-19 2020 edition. Like many people, I spent 2020-21 socially isolated, much of it for me in St. Mary's Hospital at Mayo Clinic. About this time last year, a nasty infection inside a cardiac device, implanted to keep me alive after a bad heart attack in 2016, almost put me down for keeps.

Through the generosity of an anonymous organ donor, I received a heart transplant at the end of October 2021. Going on ten months transplanted now, the worst of the anti-rejection medication side-effects behind me, I'm feeling better than I have in years. Or I was.

Two weeks ago, a common virus lurking in my donor heart suddenly woke up and began expressing itself by kicking me and my compromised immune system in the teeth. Once again, wonderful healthcare providers, including my wife Beth, are pulling me off the drain, allowing me to stay at home and get some office hours in, while daily, hour-long infusions of an IV med I still cannot pronounce has time to work its magic.

Before CM virus, I was still digging myself out of the hole that long hospitalizations, infection, a couple of operations, and drug side-effects dropped me into. I'm still climbing up to the surface through book and magazine submissions, books in progress, acquisitions, contracts, editing and design projects. Oh—and accounting.

Makes for a pretty good excuse I suppose—being so far behind on Shipwreckt priorities. *Folk Opera* has remained on top of the to-do list since I first laid out a draft galley in December '21. Even in my recovery fog, I believed this magazine is a valuable resource, a place for emerging and established writers to mingle. I apologize to all the contributors to this issue for having predicted a dozen different release dates. I know how frustrating constant delays can be. On the other hand, thanks to tremendous contributors, *Lost Lake Folk Opera n7* is now out of the gate. Thank you all for your support and patience. This issue provides a sampling of some great essayists, playwrights, poets, and writers of short fiction.

It's important for *Folk Opera* to continue. The mag has grown through eleven issues over ten years to become a unique literary magazine where good journalism and honest, civil opinion ranks in stature alongside great fiction, poetry, and plays.

This issue spotlights a group of talented writers from Northfield, Minnesota, where, with the help of Northfield Poet Laureate, Rob Hardy, a regional literary renaissance has been taking place. Rob's dedication to promoting the literary arts in schools, among adult writers and readers, in bookstores, restaurants, bars, public spaces, videos, and on social media is worthy of note.

Illiberal Democracy, the focus of this special issue, is hard to stick a fork into; it's slippery. Many of the author, playwright and poet contributors explore facets of Democracy's dark fish from different angles. I write this during a week of primaries, the week that the DOJ issued a warrant for the FBI to search the Mar a Lago residence of Donald Trump. My friends, there is at once so much to digest, and yet practically nothing left to chew on. Time for some exercise after getting fat on the months-old cold chowder we've been fed. Get up. Stand up. Act like Democracy depends on you.

Winona
August 2022

nto Focus: Horror scenes. Cities burning. Somewhere, a downtown burns. St. Louis, burning. A bonfire, more flames. In NW Portland, just flames. New Orleans, flames, too. In Boston, Snatch and Grab. People running in all directions. **Blackout**. *Gunfire.*

Louis Armstrong kisses his autographed Henri Selmer B-flat trumpet.
A Blues Voice:
Cities burning, cities burning
Get the engines, get the engines.
Fire, fire! People dying!
Fetch some water. Get some water.
Put it out. Now, I'm on fire,
Put me out, now; put me out!"
A white man in a black suit sings, "*Nes gadol haya sham*."
A black woman in a white dress answers, singing, "A great miracle happened there."
Blackout.
 A teletype clacks into life.
"News Update,"
It clacks on, prints.
—"Sole fatality is black."
A black man dragged behind a truck, loses his footing,
Screams, falls, first on his knees, then onto his back,
As the truck drives on, (dragging him behind belching trucks,
Jews once upon a time, are dragged on Germany's gingerbread
streets). Running, falling on their knees, they are dragged on;
Al Jolson is singing "Mammy" in blackface.
Hitler is sawing the air with his hand,
Blacks and Jews react!—forming a leering,
spitting crowd—left, right, left, right—
Men wail, dragged on by the trucks.

From somewhere else, we hear "Strange Fruit."
We see—we see a sycamore tree.
A black face swings into sight, a lurching pendulum,
hanging from a limb, Eyes bulging— look!

A real *risus sardonicus* there, the smile of the
    dead—
An old Jew, anointed with gasoline from a
jerrycan, whimpers, "Hear me, Israel, the Lord
our God is the one God."
A match is tossed, and a "whoosh" of gasoline
ignites.

The crowd cheers easily.
A voice asks: "Can a short story be too tragic
for its length?"
Answering, we hear, "More tragic than what's
too tragic, boy?"
"Than the tragic of swinging on a sycamore
tree!" *Laughter.*
"Than opinions enumerated, minions,
changing,
covering, weaving like Mohammed Ali,
Fixing expectations, unlike pendular motion,
Identical numerators, not of seconds, year to
year,
But denominators change."
Tick—look away—tock—try to look stolid—
With a respectable formula, painful repetition,
pedestrian math
preserving perceived pain; what horror is an
acceptable ratio?
 Science asks us: Without baked blackbirds,
will the value of pi disappear?
If gray is washed from blackbirds' blackboards,
does only black remain?
"O Little Town of Bethlehem" plays on a carillon,
A church steeple rises within curls of smoke.
Little girls in white, giggle, kneel at a chancel rail,
Which explodes, leaving no little girls, no white,
Just red stains on a chancel rail, and red streaked
dresses.
Grab the black man walking in a public square.
Chain him to a pickup truck and drive!
Troll him like a fishing lure.
When the truck shifts gears, he'll run.
Drop him, drag him on his knees,
When he struggles to stand. The truck speeds
up,
And when the driver shifts,

The black man flips, flounder-like, onto his
back.
The truck stops. Some pour gasoline on the
black man,
While other white guys fight to toss a lighted
match.
"~~Niggercide~~," they laugh, as if *anycide* is a cide too
light.
One of death's pale pals cracks jokes, lights up
a "roller,"
Tosses his lit match, **and the black man
screams.** Flames!
The white men laugh, incinerating human's
dreams
of freedom, happiness and life.
So he goes silent, free at last, at least he's silent.
But one last effort; he mouths the word "free"
and is no more.
In silence, a susurration—breath.
Attending such transactions, a hanging or a
cookout,
 They say, "He's a gambler, a murderer; an
honest thief."
So is this mob of hanging, burning yesterdays;
Innocent or guilty, but ravaged by mob law;
and on it goes;
Till all defended walls are breached or
disregarded.
Is the wingspan of Evil smaller than a man?
Unpunished, may the lawless preach violence
unrestrained?
"Government is the deadly bane, celebrating its
suspension,
Praying "God grant that we annihilate our
foes." Good men
Gladly spill their blood to claim their desires,
maybe theirs,
Cheering for destroyed property, families and
lives.
Disgusted by a Government that offers no
protection,
They fight, themselves, chewing off their own
limbs,
Thinking, save nourishment, they have nothing
to lose.

Mobocracy destroys the house built with blood—
Even its own. We the People breathe Government, suffer much,
endure evils long and patiently, and invite the enemy in.
Yet, when laws are despised, ignored,
When the right to be secure in one's person and property
Is lost in the caprice of the Mob;
Its consequence alienates us from Government.
Sooner or later it all comes to that.

The mob does not redress grievances. It only takes.
…Is it unreasonable to expect that someone
With enough ambition to stretch the gift to its utmost
Will someday spring up among us?
And if such a one does, will the people come together,
To attach government to law, intelligently,
Successfully to frustrate the pressures of the Mob?
Distinction will be the Hero's sole objective,
And though he would acquire it to do either good or harm;
When the opportunity is past, with nothing to be built up,
He will boldly pull-down what invaders never could,
With the silent artillery of false conviction
Leveling walls with wrong belief.
The forest of our giant native oaks is gone;
The unremitting hurricane of talk swept them all away,
Leaving only, here and there, a lonely trunk,
A hint of green—a shadow of foliage

Unshading and Unshaded, whistling in the hot wind,
To enter combat with mutilated limbs, to storm,
Subside, and be no more.
Reason—calculating, cold, holy as a Jesuit, and flat,
Must furnish all support and all defense.
—Let material be molded with *intelligence, morality*,
And reverence for our Constitution and her laws:
Let it be said that we tried, up to the last moment;
That we remained free, and steadfast, to the last instant;
That we revered His name, to the last breath;
That, during the sleep of centuries,
We let no hostile foot desecrate our land;
And that when the last trumpet calls us all to reveille,
Our heroes shall again awaken to defend our land.

A bass voice commands, "Let freedom ring!"
A little girl innocently lisps, "*and no demon Vomited from the gates of hell shall sojourn in our land.*"
"Not for long!" a man chimes in. "Prepare!"
"Raise the flag, beat the drum, bugler blow taps!"
  Prepare to make the noise of battle now,
to cover the tracks of traitors,
And Mourn, mourn, mourn, for our Republic is moribund,
And Liberty may die without the ability
to argue and choose wrong.

FADE TO BLACK

Anthony S. Heck

Sister's Hand to Hold

rina bounded into the house, her lanky limbs shoving past Lilly into the pantry. When Trina saw her mom's car missing from the driveway, she knew to attack the cookies. Lilly had the housekey though, so Trina had been forced to wait in fervent excitement to obtain her treat. Their mom had been late a few times this past month, and the girls suspected their dad and mom were getting back together. Though this would be the fourth time, each joinder of the family gave them hope for permanence. When the family stayed together, a blissful correlation grew in family game nights, movie binges, and cooking together, yet the most recent fallout between their parents had left the girls huddled and crying, as Mom screamed for Dad to leave once more.

"Trina! Don't eat more than four, or Mom will get mad. Plus, you'll throw up, and I'm not cleaning it."

"Yes, you will," Trina said, crumbs of an Oreo cookie fluttering from her mouth. "You can't stand leaving a mess out for Mom. She'll blame you anyway, since you're older." Trina stuck out her chocolate laced tongue, reaching in the container for another cookie.

Lilly set her bookbag on the kitchen counter, taking out her homework. "Did you get any homework?"

"No."

"Let me see."

"No."

"You probably have homework if you won't let me see."

"I don't."

Lilly snatched Trina's backpack from the kitchen floor. She opened Trina's work assignment folder to both math and reading homework.

"You lied," Lilly said, shaking the papers in front of her sister.

"I don't want to do it right now. Can't we watch television until Mom gets home?"

"I think we should do our homework. That way we don't have to upset Mom. If she brings Dad over, then we can have more time with them." Trina grabbed another cookie. Lilly reached for the bag, but Trina pulled back. Lilly dropped the papers, grabbed Trina's arm, then swiped the container. "You can have these when you're done. It won't take more than twenty minutes."

Trina started crying, banging her fist on the counter. "No fair, Lilly. You aren't the boss of me."

"Remember I'm older, and when Mom isn't here, I'm the boss. Come on."

"Fine," Trina said, sighing, collapsing on the table.

Lilly picked up the dropped papers and placed them in front of Trina. She made sure to keep the cookies next to her, as her sister would spend more time trying to sneak them away than focusing on her work. Lilly took out her own homework, frustrated that sixth grade required all the additional effort.

She hated junior high with its chaos of different teachers and rush between classes. She missed the stalwart order of elementary school.

"It's fine. Mom will be home any minute."

"Maybe, we should call Grandma."

"No. I'm sure Mom will be home soon. If we call Grandma now, she'll only worry."

Trina's face puckered, as she began to cry. She despised adults telling her how to behave, but she did not like this feeling of being unprotected.

Lilly's focus drifted, wishing her mom left a note. Whenever her mother intended on coming home late, she always left a note telling them when she would be home. The absence scared Lilly, but she could not let Trina know. Trina would panic and cry, leaving Lilly in a worse situation.

Trina focused on her multiplication, easily moving through her five times table. When she encountered her spelling words, she began banging her head. She despised reading, or at least the assigned reading by Mr. Roster. He never allowed them to have fun books of flying carpets and dragons. Everything centered on children in ridiculous predicaments that bored her by the second page.

"Can I take a break?"

"No."

"Why?"

"Because Mom will get stressed out."

"I want a cookie," Trina said, sticking her hand out. "I did my math work."

"One cookie, and then you finish your reading."

Lilly brought out the cookie. Trina grabbed and gobbled it, causing her to choke for a moment before swallowing.

"Did you even taste it?" Lilly said with disgust.

"Do your homework," Trina mimicked, rolling her eyes down to the word beautiful, trying to work through the next ten pages so she could answer the stupid questions. Trina glared at the book, digesting the material with capable speed when she focused. Two sentences written down for each question about some girl having a fight with some boy about a dog. She knew more specifics but did not care to recall them.

"I'm done," Trina said, clapping her hands. "Give me the cookies. I'm watching television."

Lilly eyed her sister, looking down at the twenty more math problems before her. She considered quitting but immediately felt guilty at the idea. She was meant to take care of the house in her mother's absence, including completing homework. She tossed the container of cookies on the table. Trina snatched them, running into the living room.

"If you make a mess, you're cleaning it," Lilly yelled.

Trina ignored her bothersome sister, turning on cartoons, losing herself in the bizarre passions of fairies, underwater creatures, and loosely held dramatics. Lilly trudged through her final math problems. She tried to pretend she did not miss her mother by focusing on the tangible problem before her. Every time her mother's car was not in the driveway, she felt a surge of panic that something may have happened. She knew she could call Grandma or Aunt Cindy, but both would bother Mom about leaving the kids alone. Mom never yelled at Lilly, but she knew the look of disappointing sadness after her mom got off the phone defending herself, pointing out Lilly's grown-up attitude and ability to care for Trina. Lilly did not want her mother to know the terror she felt at being alone, only eleven years old, with a seven-year-old sister that needed to fight over everything.

Once Lilly completed her schoolwork, the clock neared five in the evening. Disappointed, she knew that Mom would be home late, requiring her to make dinner for Trina and herself. Mom either made it home an hour after school or showed up right before bedtime with apologies, hugs, kisses, and the sweet smell of wine on her breath. Though annoyed, Lilly still loved the gleeful way Mom praised her when she came home at those late-night hours. She looked over to Trina giggling. She sighed, going into her room to take a nap.

Trina marveled over the intricacies of color, the vividness of the make-believe characters placed in everyday situations, or even better, fighting some magical demon or arcane villain. The hours ticked by as she munched on her cookies, keeping a firm gaze at the screen. When one of her most hated shows about children in school appeared, she looked around for her sister, alarmed at the unlit rooms throughout the house; darkness crept into the late-night hour.

"Lilly," she screamed. "Lilly!" Trina ran to her sister's room, shaking her sister awake from her bed.

"What?" Lilly said, fighting to keep her eyes shut.

"Mom's still not home, and it's dark."

Lilly jerked awake, looking at her alarm clock, just past eight. Where was their mother?

Adults had abilities, a defense through responsibility. She looked upon her sister, not feeling the same security. Despite Lilly's bossiness, she was still a little girl just as much as Trina.

"Why don't we make dinner? Won't that make you feel better?"

Trina shook her head vehemently. "It's too dark," she wailed.

"Well, we'll turn every light on in the house," Lilly said, hurrying out of bed to turn on both lights in her room. "There. Now we can turn on all the others."

"Won't Mom get mad," Trina whimpered.

"She's not here, so I don't see how. Come on. Let's see who can turn on the most lights the fastest." Lilly motioned as if she was going to run out of the room, letting Trina sprint into the living room to turn on the lamps, giggling at the race. Lilly was relieved that her sister's mood had turned so quickly at such a silly game. Now that the little crisis had been averted, she began having her own reservations about her mother's absence. She battled over calling their grandmother. Lilly breathed in deep, knowing she could care for Trina until their mother arrived. Outside her room, lights dazzled in all areas of the house. She turned into the bathroom, flipping on the only light that seemed remaining.

"You've won," Lilly yelled out.

"Should I turn on the porch light?" Trina called from the kitchen.

"If you want." Lilly knew her mother would be disappointed in all the electricity being used, but she could not fathom her mother's objection when she left her two children alone at night. She wished her mom thought of her more, understanding that placing such burdens on her caused her anxiety in a daily reproach. She never seemed to know what to expect from either of her parents anymore.

Trina bounded to the living room to turn on the front porch light. She pushed aside the beige curtain to peak out the large bay window. Despite the bright beacon, she could only see the array of brush and trees surrounding the small roadway to the house. Not even the neighbors across the road were visible through the lush landscape. Mom had been adamant in moving to the countryside to allow the girls the benefit of the natural world. Trina had been upset that her trip to school took fifteen minutes longer, until she saw that her bedroom was twice as big. Dad remained in their apartment in town, so she visited her old home a few times a month, yet this sprawling ranch house soon became the signature of home that Trina loved. The old apartment was now monikered as 'Dad's place.'

Lilly glided beside Trina. "What do you see? Is something out there?"

"No. Just looking."

"Do you want to make dinner?"

"I'm not very hungry," Trina said, twitching her nose.

"That's because you are full of cookies. You aren't feeling sick?"

Trina shook her head, then turned to scope out the countryside once more. A twinge of panic began again, as she could not recall sleeping at the house without an adult. This renewed feeling caused her chest to throb as sobs escalated.

Lilly rolled her eyes, wrapping her arms around her little sister. Trina's auburn hair, identical to her own, crinkled in Lilly's nose. The sisters had developed all their mother's looks: long nose, short-framed mouth, and lanky extremities. The only inheritance from their father seemed to be his array of freckles over his face. Trina pushed her face into Lilly's shoulder.

"Want me to braid your hair?" Lilly said.

"What?" Trina sputtered.

"I can braid your hair if you want. Like Mom does. I've been practicing with my friends at school."

"Okay," Trina said, wiping her nose on her arm.

"That's disgusting," Lilly said, grabbing a tissue from the coffee table and handing it to Trina. Trina wiped her arm without fuss. "I'm going to make a sandwich. Why don't you pick a movie for us both to watch, while I braid your hair?"

"Any movie I want," Trina said, looking devilish to Lilly.

"Sure, as long as it's not a grown-up movie."

"But Lilly," Trina whined. "You said any movie."

"You know I meant any movie Mom would let us watch."

"Fine," Trina said, shoving her head into the couch cushions.

Lilly sighed, heading to the kitchen, reflecting over her options. She could make a peanut butter sandwich with little trouble. Her mother had been adamant about her keeping away from the stove, so she did not dare make any hot meal. She looked in the freezer for temptation, eyeing the chicken tenders. She considered microwaving but despised the soggy breading. She brushed the ice cream but decided to save it for a snack later, when Trina fell asleep. She grabbed the supplies: bread, knife, peanut butter, and forged her dinner.

Trina flipped through the channels, passing a *Harry Potter* movie, some horror movie regarding a clown, artsy films she did not recognize, until she settled on *Garfield: The Movie*. She did not have a special love for Garfield, but she enjoyed the lazy, fat kitty, reminding her of a pet she wished she could own. Mom had allergies to both cats and dogs, or so she claimed. Trina had peppered dog hair, that she obtained from her friend Patty's labradoodle, throughout the house including her mom's bed. Her mom expressed some frustration at the surprising wisps of hair, but Trina never saw her mom sneeze. She told Lilly, but Lilly told her to let it go, that they would not get a dog either way.

"Are you almost done? Garfield is about to start," Trina yelled.

"I'm coming." Lilly hurried with two peanut butter sandwiches and a glass of juice, placing them on the coffee table.

"Did you make me one?" Trina said.

"You said you weren't hungry."

"Now I am."

"Fine. Take one of the sandwiches."

Trina bounced up, eyeing each sandwich. She took a quick bite of the one with more peanut butter. "Thank you," she said with a full mouth.

"That's disgusting. Shut your mouth."

Trina shrugged, chomping on her sandwich once more.

"Sit in front of me. I can do your hair from the sofa." Trina scooted between her sister's legs, finishing up the sandwich.

"Did you even chew?"

"Yes," Trina said, annoyed at her sister's nagging. "Quiet. The movie's on."

The sisters sat together, laughing in tandem at the shenanigans Garfield, John, and Odie found themselves. Lilly tried her best to draw Trina's hair into pigtails, inadvertently pulling too hard a second time. Trina jerked away and slapped Lilly's leg, believing Lilly tried to purposely torture her. Lilly apologized, her voice cracking, claiming she was doing her best. Trina apologized, pushing herself back into position. Lilly eased her grip, but this caused the pigtails to come out loose and uneven. She thought to tell Trina that she could do better if Trina would sit still and allow her to keep the hair taught, but Lilly did not have the energy. As the movie ended and ten o'clock encroached upon them, Lilly turned off the television, telling Trina to go to bed.

"Why don't you have to go to bed, too?" Trina whined, though she felt the reign of exhaustion pulling upon her.

"You are supposed to be in bed by nine. I let you stay up. Mom will be furious if you aren't asleep."

"Mom's not here," Trina said, sticking her tongue out.

"I know," Lilly said quietly.

"We should call Grandma."

"No," Lilly said in earnest. "I don't want her mad at Mom. She'll be in bed anyway."

"We can call the police. Isn't that what Mom told us to do if we got scared, and she wasn't around."

"We aren't in danger, Trina. Police don't just come over and stay the night."

"I don't know," Trina said, her lip puckered.

"Let's just keep watching movies. Here. You can lay down on the couch."

"Did you lock the doors?"

Panic coursed through Lilly, as she rushed to the front and back doors. The back door had been locked, but anyone could have come through the front door. She flipped the deadbolt and lock on the doorknob to little relief. Trina watched Lilly's erraticism with earnest.

"Can we watch the *Tale of Two Kitties*?" Trina said, as Lilly studied the door. Lilly could not shake that feeling of dread now that it had been released.

"What's that?" Lilly said offhanded.

"The second Garfield movie. It's playing right now."

"Sure," Lilly said. She looked to the dining room table chairs, then to the sofa chair nearest the door. She wanted to block the door in some way but did not know what to place before the door that would be heavy enough. The couch. They could push it against the door and still watch television from it, though the viewing would be skewed from the right.

"Help me push the couch against the door."

"Why?"

"Just help me."

Lilly heaved against the couch, little movements with each effort against the carpet. Trina tried pushing from the cushion side to even the couch with the door, but she did not have any influence. "Push with me, Trina." Together, the girls were able lean the couch against the door. Lilly wiped the sweat off her face; her troubling stomach easing its ferocity.

"Can we watch the movie now?" Trina said, hopping on the couch without a response.

Lilly pulled over the sofa chair next to the couch, trying to focus on the movie. As she expected, Trina fell asleep within minutes. Lilly turned off the movie and began streaming *Pretty Little Liars* before drifting off herself.

A flick on the window caused Lilly to stir, pushing herself from the chair. Her neck ached from falling asleep in the chair. She crept to the window to see what made the noise. A few branches rustled from a wind vortex with no strangers ready to accost their home. Lilly went to the kitchen to check the back door, still locked. She blinked at the time, just past two in the morning. She considered waking Trina and

guiding her to bed. However, Lilly worried Trina would panic, and she was too tired to be any more accommodating. She stumbled toward the hallway, when she heard another crack on the window from the living room. She tip-toed to the window, looking out for the villain.

Ghostly moans escaped from the trees, as the leaves rustled and fell from the onslaught of wind. A part of her wanted to step outside, verify that no one lurked among the noises, but this would require Trina's help in moving the couch. The idea of stepping outside from the backdoor traipsed through her mind, but she did not have the courage to run around through the dark. Inside these confines she had some semblance of safety. She pressed her face to the glass; eyes quivering for any movement aside from nature's torrent. A branch slammed against the window, causing her to scream out. In chorus, Trina screamed out of fright due to her sister's outburst. Neither tired until Lilly began coughing. Trina ran to her sister, hugging her tightly.

"What's going on?" Trina wailed. "Why did you scream?"

Lilly tried to speak but pointed to the sprawling crack in the window. Thankfully, the branch had not penetrated the glass for Lilly knew she would have been severely hurt. She began crying, unsure whether she was still scared or just relieved.

"Lilly," Trina said, pulling on her shirt. "Lilly, please."

"I'm fine," Lilly croaked. "I got scared when the branch hit the window."

Trina then noticed the spiderweb of cracks, amazed by the damage. She reached out to touch the lines, but Lilly pulled her hand back. "Don't. You could still get cut." Trina harrumphed, crossing her arms. "Go to bed," Lilly said. "I'll stay out here and keep watch."

"Keep watch of what?" Trina whispered.

"I don't know. There's a storm, I think."

Trina rolled her eyes, "You need to watch the storm?"

"No. Well, I don't know if someone else is out there. You go on to bed, and I'll stay up."

"How are you going to protect us?"

Lilly looked around, realizing that she had no means of fighting off potential burglars. "I could get a knife."

"Doesn't Mom have a gun under her bed?"

"Yeah, but we aren't to touch it."

Trina walked into her mother's room, pulling out the gun case. Lilly hurried after her, placing her foot on it. The touch gave her a small feeling of power, that the contents would truly fight off any bad guy. Trina pushed Lilly's foot away, opening the case. Trina tried to pull up the butt of the gun, but Lilly slapped her hand away.

"Hey. No hitting."

"You shouldn't touch it. I can hold the gun on the couch, while you go to bed."

"That's no fair," whined Trina. "I want to protect the house, too." She stomped her feet, frustrated by her big sister's incessant bossiness.

Lilly ignored her, admiring the gun with its chestnut-colored bottom that gave off a walnut smell like the trees outside, the cool, sleek charcoal barrel, and small trigger point that would make the whole machine explode. She took the gun out of the case, careful not to point the barrel at Trina. "We can both sit on the couch and watch for bad guys, okay? Just don't get in front of the gun. You hear me? Don't touch the trigger or get in front of the gun."

"Okay," Trina said, hopping to the couch.

Lilly slung the gun in front of her, careful to hold the barrel facing down to the floor away from her feet. A strange nervousness came upon her. She was afraid of hurting someone with the weapon but felt comfort with it in her hands. She directed Trina to sit in the middle of the couch, while she plumped some pillows on the armrest, scooting to the couch edge away from the door.

"Now, you come in closer between my legs and bring the gun up over you."

As Trina tried to find a comfortable way for the gun to lay upon her, she grew frustrated, hurling herself off the couch. Lilly panicked, as Trina came before the barrel of the gun.

"What are you doing?"

"This isn't working, Lilly. I'm going to bed."

Trina stomped off into her bedroom without explanation. Lilly, relieved at her sister's moment of lucidity, pulled a pillow between her legs, so she could easily rest the gun facing the front door. Moments later, she fell asleep to the whippings of the wind.

Lilly heard rustling but refused to acknowledge the noise. Exhausted, she could not believe that she was being waken so early.

"I can't believe you have a gun, Sherry."

"I have a gun to protect myself. What did you think I would do moving out into the country by myself, Bill? I'm a woman alone in the woods. There's no bullets in it. They are locked in a small safe in my closet, so calm down."

"Even so," the man muttered.

Lilly felt a pull on the gun. She woke with ferocity, holding the gun tightly, reaching for the trigger.

"Lilly. Lilly. Calm down, baby. It's only me. Daddy."

Lilly eased her grip, blinking enough to see the shape of her father before her. He gently pulled the gun away, walking into Mom's room. Her mother then came around, guiding Lilly into her room, laying her down to bed.

"Why didn't you call Grandma?" her mom asked.

"I didn't want you to get in trouble," yawned Lilly.

Her mother kissed her on the forehead. "You took real good care of your sister. I'm proud of you."

"Where were you?"

"You'll be so happy, baby," her mom said, sitting next to her. "Your father and I got married." She displayed her ring in Lilly's face.

Lilly turned her body away, curling up. She began to drift off once more, finding peace.

Ellen Thompson

The Lion—Two Sonnets

Not in This Life

We'll never see it eye to eye, my friend,
As hard as we may try, it's not to be.
I'm weary of my acts I must defend,
A solitude I crave, away from thee...

When fire collides with fire, the end is clear –
A pile of ashes is their churning path.
And though we are to shed a bitter tear,
The greener for its moisture is the grass.

The seasons change, emotions spark and die.
A tree is lighter when the winter comes.
The summer bids the spring a firm goodbye.
The autumn follows with its rainbow drums.
Like seasons, we can never stay the same.
In moving on with time, are we to blame?

The Lion

In Kenya I was running, free and wild,
the picture of a contumacious beast—
My luck pursued me since I was a child,
To such as I, the world was one big feast.

I lived and loved and, yes, I killed for fun;
My teeth devoured a roe's delightful flesh.
Poor dears, their lot was always on the run,
but in the end, their meat was soft and fresh.

The king of beasts I was until one day—
don't ask me how—in California zoo
I ended up, a scarecrow, shamed, dismayed,
for crowds' amusement and the keepers' too.

And now my body, stuffed, alive no more
is on display in East Coast jewelry store.

Sweet Snack Recipe

sweet snack recipe:

five (5) sets of pre-packaged peanut butter cheese crackers
one (1) bottle of water

unwrap your first set of peanut butter cheese crackers. there should be four (4) in each plastic skin.

put your first peanut butter cheese cracker in your mouth. the crackers are cheddar cheese flavored & the filling is peanut butter.

the cracker will be salty dry at first so you will take a nice big swig of water from your water bottle. the sweetness of the peanut butter will be highlighted among the not-dry taste of the crackers.

you will eat these repeatedly every day until you get sick of them. you have never even bought these in real life.

you only own these crackers because your college gives them away for free. you have no grocery money this week & it's finals & you're a senior trying to graduate.

when you are done eating you will throw away all your peanut butter cheese cracker wrappers. you will then put away all the peanut butter cheese crackers that you didn't eat. just like those granola bars that you hate but you eat them anyway.

thirsty.

Fancy Chocolates

for my mom's birthday this year
i bought her

four (4) boxes
of dollar store fancy chocolates

because that was the best i could do
under my budget

& she loves
fancy treats.

my mom's birthday
is two days before christmas

& i'm probably going to
be working that day

just like
christmas eve
christmas day
new year's eve
new year's day

so i stow away the stash
of presents
in a shelf in my room

ready to be wrapped
later

but not quite now

& i don my
santa hat
& christmas sweater

every day of this
december.

my mom grew up poor
in the oregon countryside

& she says
when she was a kid

christmas & birthdays
really weren't a big deal

but she would still get upset
when people would forget her birthday
& try to pull that
it counts for both nonsense.

for my mom's birthday this year
i bought her

four (4) boxes
of dollar store fancy chocolates

wrapped in birthday paper
instead of green & red

& i don't know when
i'll give it to her

but delicate delights
set in nice boxes

always seem
to bring her joy.

Four (4) Dozens of Eggs

my dad said he noticed
that my minifridge had
four (4)
dozens of eggs.

& i said
dad i told you not to snoop through my things
he said
it was only your fridge
i'm just proud of you
for eating eggs so much.

which i think is funny
because every breakfast he ever served me
was always scrambled eggs
& i hated them so much
that i never touched eggs.

so instead i have mastered
soft boiled eggs
upon cheap ramen

& sunny side up
inside my own version
of an egg mcmuffin
as inspired by a close friend
who died over (2) years ago.

i only enjoy
scrambled eggs
with sharp cheddar, butter, & pepper
in the way that my best friend
makes them.

funny how
so many of my friends
have relation
to simply eating eggs.

because yes i hate scrambled
but probably just the way that my dad makes them.

i think it's funny
that when my dad looks in my fridge
the fist thing he notices

is eggs.

One (1) Big Apple

one (1) big apple
eaten lonely from
all this great big banquet of food.

the crunch
is sweet.
& the juice
hydrates tongue.

ruby red
this apple shines
with just a patch
of sunrise yellow
grown in a great big family
of seeds

the apple
doesn't fall far
from the tree.

& the poison
of witches

is not found
in cyanide seeds

because cyanide seeds
need to grow

into cyanide trees.

& from a great big orchard
grows all the red vessels
of fruit.

apple seeds
taste like almonds.
& so johnny appleseed
takes this great big handful of apple seeds

& grows them in
one (1) flower pot
in his room.

on his birthday
he shall eat
a nice big bowl
of apple seeds

for his room
has become crowded
with apples

because the giving tree
could only give so much.

one (1) big apple
eaten lonely from
all this great big banquet of food.

the crunch
is sweet.
& the juice
hydrates tongue.
& Spray All Your Filth

when i tell you
please put on your mask
& you scream
fuck you

in my face
at the top of your lungs
in front of your children

& storm off maskless anyway

some of us
have friends
who have died
from disease

when you scream
fuck you

& spray
all your filth

some of us
know it's better
to be mildly inconvenienced

instead of having another time
where one of your closest friends
is found dead
in a los angeles apartment

i know you think
they don't work
but some of us
are just trying
to work minimum wage jobs
to survive

when others
couldn't go to the emergency room
in time
& doctors are expensive

could you please
shut the fuck up
you spoiled prick
& just put on your stupid mask

some of us
have bigger problems
than cloth.

Sean Murphy

Memory is a Thief

**C**haracters: **Conrad:** An older man. He's been living on the streets a long time. **Whalen:** Younger. The personification of a violent memory that haunts **Conrad**, a melody stuck in the head.

Scene: Under a bridge on a rainy night.
Time: Refuses to pass.

Setting: *It is raining.* **Conrad** *and* **Whalen** *are under a bridge.* **Whalen** *lurks on the edge of the light and just out of the rain playing "Conversation with Death" on a fiddle.* **Conrad** *is sitting on an old couch. In front of him is a small wooden crate with a candle burning on it.* **Conrad** *slowly and methodically takes pills one at a time out of various prescription bottles, swallowing them each with a sip from a tall can of Budweiser.*

Conrad: *Yelling.* Ghost.

Whalen: *Continues playing.* **Conrad** *Takes more pills.*

Conrad: Stupid ghost. **Whalen** *continues playing.* **Conrad** *takes even more pills.*

Conrad: *Raising voice.* You're not funny. I'm not laughing.

Whalen: *Stops playing.*

Conrad: Are you real? I thought I was imagining you. Don't lurk. If you're real, come out.

Whalen: *Approaches.*

Conrad: You are real. Well, don't fiddle around then. Come over here and get dry. I won't bite. You're not really a ghost, are you? *Gestures at the couch.* You picked a bad night to be out busking.

Whalen: *Takes seat on couch as far away from* **Conrad** *as possible.*

Conrad: That's good. You stay over there. I don't want you to get too close to me either. One beer. One beer a night. Who the hell can get a wink of sleep out on the street without at least one beer?

Conrad *passes* **Whalen** *a can of beer.* **Whalen** *puts it in a pocket and stands up.*

Conrad: I'd feel safer if you stayed for a while. After the pills, I drift off. Just keep an eye on me for a bit. I paid for your fiddle music, didn't I? You're going to keep that beer. You know it will help you sleep.

Whalen: Looks pensively to the they'd emerged from.

Conrad: You might be a ghost, huh? You don't talk. Play something, though. You play good.

Whalen: *Plays a lullaby.*

Conrad: Kiki. Kiki's gone. You don't know. You're new around here. I could sleep when Kiki was here. If you don't want people to take your stuff. Get a dog.

Conrad: D*rifts off.* **Whalen** *stops playing and watches* **Conrad** *sleep.* **Whalen** *takes a seat next to* **Conrad.** **Conrad** *wakes briefly.*

Conrad: You're a very gentle person, aren't you?

Whalen: *waits to be sure* **Conrad** *is asleep again before quietly searching* **Conrad's** *backpack and pocketing a handful of bills.*

Conrad: I can't ever sleep more than a few minutes at a time. These pills are supposed to help me stay asleep. But I can't take those. If I took those, I would be dead to the world for hours. They'd rob me blind. Don't trust anybody out here on the street. Get a dog. You can trust a dog.

Conrad *pauses. After a moment of reflection, he continues.* I grew up in a nice house, you know. Up on the west side. My father was a doctor.

Whalen: Bad things happen in nice houses.

Conrad: Yeah.

Whalen: I can't sleep indoors. Can you?

Conrad: No. Anything can happen behind a closed door. I like to be out here where everybody can see what's going on.

Whalen: It's easier to trust ten people than it is to trust one, right?

Conrad: When was the last time you ate?

Conrad *takes bread fixings out of bag and makes* **Whalen** *a sandwich.*

Conrad: Look at this. Oatmeal bread. *Uses a squeeze packet of mayonnaise, a slice of swiss cheese, some green olives and pepper from a packet.* You gotta have pepper. You keep looking at me like I'm the Christmas goose. Eat. Drink that beer.

Whalen: *Takes sandwich, opens the beer, and hungrily consumes both.*

Conrad: *Singing and falling back to sleep.*

Pretty Susie she came by
With a book under her arm.

She walked up to her true love's grave
And she began to charm.
She charmed the fish out of the sea
And the birds out of their nests.
She charmed her true love out of his grave
So he could no longer rest.
Will you go to the rolling of the stones?
Or the dancing of the ball?
Or will you go and see pretty Susie
And dance among them all?

Conrad *falls asleep.* **Whalen** *finishes eating.* **Whalen** *cautiously continues searching* **Conrad's** *belongings, taking what they find valuable, while* **Conrad** *sleeps.*

Whalen: *Collects his fiddle and readies to leave but stops first to tuck a blanket around* **Conrad.**

Conrad: Stupid ghost. I still see it, you know?

Whalen: Who is it? Who do you see?

Conrad: My little brother. You look like him.

Whalen: I look like a lot of people. Who hurt him?

Conrad: Our dad.

Whalen: The doctor.

Conrad: I just want it to be over. But he won't stay dead. Jimmy won't stay dead.

Whalen: How long has it been?

Conrad: 50 years.

Whalen: Try to sleep. I'll play again.

Whalen: *plays the fiddle.*

Emilio DeGrazia

Two Somethings to Think About

Evolutionary Tales

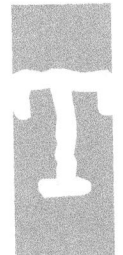he scents of things going wrong are more obviously in the air these days than any answers blowing in the wind. I learned a story about "evolution" years ago when I was a kid in the public schools. My lesson was a poster on a bulletin board. There I saw little fish-like things happily swirling in blue water, and then the picture showed them moving upward while happily growing fins. Then they magically sprouted leg-like appendages. Then, behold, they walked ashore, grew bigger and hairy, and lived in jungles, huts and villages. Eventually they built skyscrapers and one day were certain to go tripping off to Mars.

Most of my teachers probably didn't know the poster did not represent what scientists really were finding out about evolution. But the poster made it easier for everyone to feel good about the human story. It was, above all, a "Progress" story. The poster proudly displayed humanity as nature's predestined elect. We, human beings, were at the top of nature's ladder of success, the self-proclaimed stars of nature's show. Nature was quietly scheming to make winners of us. Or rather, nature was said to favor some of us, a special few, the winners smart and strong enough to put loser humans, and "lower" animals, in their proper place. My cat Milo reminds me of how wrong my old teachers were. Milo insists he has a perfect right to my favorite easy chair.

A philosopher named Herbert Spencer pushed the human progress view very hard, and for a few decades he convinced even academics it was the truth. His "Social Darwinism" claimed that the modern industrial society was evolution's top achievement.

Henry Ford liked the idea. The winners would own Ford cars. Adolph Hitler loved the idea.

The winners would own Volkswagens and be blue-eyed and blond, except him.

While I was asked to believe this story my brain was also was fattened on sports, movies and TV. Whenever one of the teams I was on won a game we used the word "great" a lot. We also used the word to describe a lot of the movies and TV shows, the steady diet of mental junk-food we were routinely fed to spice up the ads. It was easy for me to believe that what I ate up as I was growing up someday would make me great. The good guys—the he-men heroes—are fit to survive and win. The poor, cancerous, crippled, insane, frail, ugly, crooked, clueless, alienated and depressed are naturally destined to obey some "law of the jungle"—call it "evolution"—that makes losers of them. They get sicker, go away, go to jail, or get killed by he-men, and they don't have a lovely romance with a gorgeous woman destined to give birth to children destined to make all the varsity teams. In most of these stories the best and bravest—like Superman and home run hitters in huge sports stadiums on freeways far from Main Street—are lion-kings.

Those considered losers in life—like all those sperm that fail to wiggle their way successfully into an egg—seem like hordes of useless extras playing pointless roles in "evolution's" progress selection schemes. These extras are so many and so diverse—the poor, cancerous, crippled, insane, frail, ugly, crooked, clueless, alienated and depressed—that the brilliant, beautiful and fit to survive rarely make any mention of them in their credit lines.

We love success stories and their happy endings and like to call them (oxymoronically) "true stories." But the real science of evolution tells untidy tales. Biology's ways are, like all gods, strange and mysterious.

They are not easily plotted on a progress curve. Whales, elephants, tigers and lions—those top of the line beasts—are losing out. While natural selection's untidy whims quietly kick in, lion hunters have a blind spot for the target on their backs. Roaches, termites, and ticks dig in to increase and multiply, while waiting things out. Zillions of them often know enough to cooperate with tiny stuff in mud, roots and each other in order to survive. Meanwhile, king-of-the-beasts lions, down to a lonely few, have fewer places to hide. Evolution can be very cruel. Lovely small creatures good for us—bees and butterflies, for example—are quietly going the way of the dinosaurs. The cells in tiny beasts—bacteria and virus species—may prove "smarter" than all our smartphones combined. They may be the most fit to survive.

COVID and its new strains come to mind. We can't see them, so it's easy to think they don't have strange eyes and noses for us. It's actually dangerous to believe they don't exist.

While all this tiny activity is invisibly going on we like to think we're techno-savvy enough to conquer outer space without ruining or running out of garden space. What we call human progress—our "technological genius" and our "taming" and "conquest" of nature—makes us feel we're still lording it over and in control of nature. In this view nature is our slave. We can tell it what to do, and it must obey. It's a loser, compared to us.

The key to human success—call it also survival these days—maybe depends on how we treat the natural presences we have tried to harness and enslave to human use and ambition, sometimes also called greed. What emanates from our American history of slavery, for example, is the need—and opportunity—for empathy and cooperation. Our nation will likely fall apart if we continue to lord it over each other.

And nature continues to be treated like our slave. The story I learned as a kid about evolution and human progress is rather obviously in deep trouble. Today's poster art depicting evolution's real ways would be bizarre indeed. We need a better story to live by than the one in the poster I saw as a kid. Quiet and often invisible success stories normally result from empathy and cooperation. Without empathy and cooperation self-proclaimed winners make a lot of noise as they try to knock each other off. Nations becoming dictatorships experience the false version of survival of the fittest in very nasty ways.

The Rattling of Chains

When I'm too lazy to do anything but smell the roses, I'm not sure I've earned the right. I usually prefer not give my privileges much thought.

But curiosity keeps hounding me. That urge takes me into dark spaces that often make me goofy dense with more ignorance. After I follow my nose too far into the dark I sometimes feel I'm in several page-turning mysteries at once.

Curiosity's also fun, so maybe it's a blessing and a curse. I think I was born with it, the same way some people think they were born with sin.

I'm often curious about words, especially their relation to realities. One word, "freedom," is out and about a lot these days, often finding its way from narrow minds into open mouths. I have trouble making sense of that word. I once read that the word "freedom" sounds like "the rattling of chains."

I'm also curious about Humpty Dumpty, that fat egg who I have no reason to think chose to fall from a wall and thereby make a sloppy mess of his life. "When I use a word it means just what I want it to mean," poor Humpty says to clueless Alice in her Wonderland. She questions him: Can words mean so many things? "The question is," says Humpty, "is who is to be master. That is all."

Humpty seems to know, perhaps too late, that those who control the meaning of words—and the stories words tell—also control lives.

How free are we if the words we routinely use make us their pawns? Should I, for example, let people call me "lazy" or "leisurely" when I'm busy smelling the flowers? Should I allow myself to be called "curious," or "clueless," or "nosy"? If the wrong words get stuck to me they could hurt my career.

In America we like to say everyone else is "free to choose." The chains start rattling when I hear that. Did I choose to be a male or female, or some combination? Was I free to be born in America rather than Mongolia? Did I choose to be born a Christian in America rather than a Muslim in Saudi Arabia? Free to choose my skin hues or hair colors? Free of the prejudices inspired by words such as "black" and "white"? Free of parental addictions, failures and prejudices? Free to make a million bucks? Free to enjoy or hate a job that pays half that much? Free to climb a ladder of success by working overtime at minimum wage? Free to make sure those minimum wages cover food, rent, health insurance, and a beer or two? In a free enterprise system am I free of promiscuous profiteering, or the algorithms devised by strangers watching and determining my private moves online?

Am I free to ignore my crooked nose and teeth?

I'm not free to say yes to all that because something compels me to say it's wrong to lie. Radical individualists—those who think it's a natural God-given right to give themselves freewheeling license to pursue their own self-interests—think they're free to disagree.

My curiosity about "freedom" gets tied in knots when I think freedom has something to do with "choice," and the knot gets tangled when the word "choice" has the word "moral" attached to it. "Moral" usually means "thou shalt not" or "it's not permitted to do what's wrong." It means you shouldn't feel free to do anything you want. Should I be free to drive faster than speed limits allow? Free to drive when drunk? Free to be seventeen years old, not yet free to vote or drink alcohol, but free to use an AK47 during a street protest? Free to ignore "thou shalt not kill" if I'm an armed crook, police hater, or believer in capital punishment? Free to do illegal drugs? Free to avoid taxes and hide my money in foreign banks? Free to look the other way when banks launder illegal drug money? Free to charge absurdly high prices for legal drugs? Free to oppose regulations that restrict unfair business, labor and voting practices? Free to pollute the environment if there's big money

to be made doing it? Free to spread my deadly germs in a crowded room?

In the good old days we used to say we weren't free to shout, "Fire!" in a crowded room. Moral choice said "thou shalt not."

It's hard to rein freedom in if you're someone like me who believes in freedom of thought and wants to let freedoms ring musically.

Henry David Thoreau reminds me of what Thomas Jefferson said. "That Government is best which governs least." I like that. I also like what Thoreau said in response: "That Government is best which governs not at all."

But they both knew that the self-government we also call Democracy depends on self-control, and that self-control is not the same as addicted obedience to dogmatic beliefs. Self-control is best grounded in thoughtful individual moral choice but has collective and profound influence when expressed by business and political leaders. When leaders lie, we all have to endure the results. Many find moral choices useful, enabling, even relaxing. They also believe that control of selfish freedoms encourages social harmony and should be the basis for how we vote.

We like to think that animals still alive in nature are wild and free, and that their wild freedom is what enables them to survive. If animals could speak to us they'd probably want to discuss the laws of the jungle they have to obey in order to survive, and why so many of them these days are experiencing the rattling of chains.

As social creatures more critically threatened by our biases and technologies, we also seem to be trying to decide whether self-government—also called Democracy—is a human survival skill.

Don Kropp

Assassination and the Decline of Representative Government in the United States.

close look at American history books, or even Webster's Unabridged Dictionary, can be revealing. Consider our succession of presidents from Washington, Adams, Jefferson. Madison and Monroe through Ronald Reagan and you will discover interesting facts about our chosen leaders and assassination as means of striking at the foundation of Democracy by overturning the election process.

This country had sixteen presidents, until John Wilkes Booth shot and killed Abraham Lincoln. From 1776 until 1864 opponents of American policy left presidents and their administrations intact. Elections, rather than assassinations, decided who would lead the citizenry.

After Lincoln's politically motivated murder, the nation endured 141 years of intermittent violence directed at presidents and presidential candidates! Political factions have been subverting the Republic and practicing indirect elite rule ever since. When this nation was an agrarian based society, it was a lot safer to run for public office. After the Industrial Revolution and the rise of Robber Barons, the highest office became far more dangerous. Industrialists, a new kind of politician, translated their economic power into political power.

The Civil War was based on many issues besides slavery, tariffs, regionalism and States' Rights issues. The landed aristocracy of the South challenged the rising industrial leaders of the North. That social conflict resulted in the most devastating war in our history, with a massive loss of lives and property to preserve a United States. The secessionist movement failed at great cost to the post-war society, which nevertheless underwent continuous change.

Just examine the violence directed at presidents after the Civil War and the assassination of Abraham Lincoln, the sixteenth US President. James Garfield, twentieth President, was shot. William McKinley, the twenty-fifth President, was shot.

President Theodore Roosevelt was later shot but survived. He lived to use anti-trust laws and government regulation to counter the power of privately-owned corporate monopolies. Skull and Bones man Howard Taft became President without a shot being fired. Wilson, Harding. Coolidge and Herbert Hoover managed to serve out their terms without attempts on their lives.

Franklin Delano Roosevelt ran for the highest office in the land during the fifth year of the Great Depression. A single women changed the history of the United States with a motion of her hand. She saw an arm raised with a pistol aimed at then presidential candidate Roosevelt. She pushed the arm of the assassin with these results. The mayor of Chicago was killed, and four others were shot.

Roosevelt, a renowned liberal, survived to be elected. The American people would go on to reelect FDR three more times. Roosevelt started the New Deal, Social Security, and the Securities Exchange Commission, and the Civilian Conservation Corps. He imposed Government regulation on privately-owned corporations. The Works Progress Administration oversaw massive public works projects creating jobs for the unemployed. He created welfare programs and used the Keynesian principle of governmental spending to stimulate economic growth.

America's industrial elite hated Roosevelt. They saw him as a class traitor, and they feared that farmers and non-farm labor would revolt to create a Bolshevik State (like in Russia in 1917). The most powerful, richest families, 156 in all, created the American Liberty League in 1933.

These families intended to overthrow democratic government and install a fascist model state. The military refused to go along with the coup and Congress covered up the plot to protect their sponsors.

Some of these same elite families supported the fascist movements in the 1930s. Adolf Hitler gave an interview to the *Detroit News* in 1931, two years before he became the German chancellor. A large portrait of Ford hung over Hitler's desk in his Munich office.

"I regard Henry Ford as my inspiration," Hitler told the *Detroit News* reporter.[1]

Now back to assassinations and the decline of Democracy in the United States.

After nearly sixteen years in office, and overseeing the United States' victory in WWII, FDR died in office. Vice President Harry Truman became our thirty-third President. A Puerto Rican separatist tried to assassinate Truman while he resided at Blair House. A police officer and the assassin were killed. Puerto Rican separatists also attacked Members of Congress.

President Dwight Eisenhower served two terms without an attempt on his life.

Then John Kennedy won the 1960 election and was assassinated on November 23, 1963, in Dallas, Texas. During the lead up to JFK's murder, right wing billionaires, the Hunt brothers and Clint Murchison, who first owned the Dallas Cowboys, circulated fliers and ran newspaper ads accusing President Kennedy of treason, forever linking them to one among many conspiracy theories that continue to circulate about the mysterious assassination of JFK.

"The Kennedy assassination and the murder of Lee Harvey Oswald by nightclub owner Jack Ruby spawned numerous conspiracy theories. These theories allege the involvement of the CIA, the Mafia, Vice President Lyndon B. Johnson, Cuban Prime Minister Fidel Castro, the KGB, or some combination of these entities. The original FBI investigation and Warren Commission report, as well as an alleged 'benign CIA cover-up,' have led to the claim that the federal government deliberately covered up crucial information in the aftermath of the assassination. Former Los Angeles District Attorney Vincent Bugliosi estimated that a total of 42 groups, 82 assassins, and 214 people had been accused at one time or another in various conspiracy scenarios."[2]

Kennedy inherited the Vietnam conflict and the famous *Domino Theory* from Eisenhower and his Secretary of State, John Foster Dulles. Kennedy recognized the opportunity to procure rubber, tin and potential oil deposits off the coast for the US The American people however were told the Vietnam War represented a battle for freedom and democracy in Southeast Asia. Segments of the elite supported proxy war against a weak communist state because communism was always a threat to America's wealthiest, who profited from our private property economic system. Anti-communism had been a cornerstone of American foreign policy since the Russian Revolution in 1917.

But then, on Thursday November 22, 1963, Kennedy ordered a reduction of troops levels in Vietnam. On Friday he was dead. The following Monday morning, the President Lyndon Johnson canceled the withdrawal order and escalated the war, which of course profited the military industrial complex that President Eisenhower has warned about in his farewell address.

JFK's brother and Attorney General, Bobby Kennedy, ran against Lyndon Baines Johnson. Bobby was assassinated the night he won the California Primary. He was leaning toward ending the war after another Democratic candidate, Eugene McCarthy, announced that, if elected, he would the war.

Dr. Martin Luther King Jr., the national civil rights leader, was assassinated on April 4, 1968, in Memphis. He was there to support striking African American city sanitation workers. One year to the day before his assassination, MLK delivered his seminal speech condemning the Vietnam War in Memphis at Riverside Church. Riots erupted in major cities across the US on April fourth and fifth. Then in mid-summer 1967, known as the "Long, Hot Summer," saw a

---

[1] The Bridge: Michigan's nonpartisan, nonprofit news source; "Henry Ford and the Jews, the story Dearborn didn't want told," by Bill McGraw, a veteran *Detroit Free Press* reporter.

[2] WWW.wikiwand.com: "John F. Kennedy assassination conspiracy theories."

continuation of the April riots, this time racial and economic in nature, and again, in major cities a

After a decade of slaughter on both sides of the War, antiwar and civil rights protesters were on the march in major cities in our deeply divided nation.

Southern Democrat and presidential candidate, George Wallace, challenged President Johnson in 1964 and lost. In 1968, Wallace mounted a third-party challenge to LBJ's reelection. Johnson stunned America when he announced that he would not run again. Democrats chose Hubert Humphry to run against at the 1968 Democratic Convention in Chicago, badly battle scarred by antiwar protests. Third-party candidate Wallace won five southern states. Wallace continues to be the most recent third-party candidate to receive pledged Electoral College votes from any state.[3]

Elected Governor of Alabama in 1970, in 1972, Wallace ran in the Democratic presidential primaries, once again campaigning for segregation. His campaign effectively ended when Arthur Bremer shot him during a campaign stop in Maryland. Nixon, who conspiracy theorists at the time believed played a role in the assassination attempt, would eventually win reelection and Governor Wallace would remain paralyzed below the waist for the rest of his life.

The assassination attempt eliminated a powerful challenge to the Nixon presidency. As it turned out, Nixon's greatest threat was himself. His presidency ended under threat of impeachment. More officials from his administration were sent to prison than any other in the nation's history.

Next up, Gerald Ford pardoned Nixon's crimes. Ford paid for that blunder by losing the next election. The elite had wanted Ford to resign so they could put Nelson Rockefeller in power. The elites feared the possibility of a Democratic. President. But Ford chose to run.

"In 1973, the Senate Watergate Committee investigation revealed that the executive branch had directed national intelligence agencies to carry out constitutionally questionable domestic security operations. In 1974 Pulitzer Prize winning journalist Seymour Hersh published a frontpage *New York Times* article claiming that the CIA had been spying on antiwar activists for more than a decade, violating the agency's charter.1 Former CIA officials and some lawmakers, including Senators William Proxmire and Stuart Symington, called for a congressional inquiry."[4]

The Church committee began its investigation on January 21, 1975. The committee identified a wide range of intelligence abuses by federal agencies, including the CIA, FBI, Internal Revenue Service, and National Security Agency. They discovered that the CIA had overthrown foreign governments and engaged in assassination. President Ford immediately tried to stop Government agencies from violating US and international law governing its covert operations.

On September 5, 1975, Lynette "Squeaky" Fromme, a former Charley Manson cult member, tried to shoot President Ford at William Land Park in Sacramento, California. The assassination attempt failed, as did a second attempt on President Ford's life. On September 22, 1975, two weeks after Squeaky Fromme's attempt on President Ford's life, Sara Jane Moore fired a pistol at the President and missed. The failed assassination took place in San Francisco as Ford was entering the St. Francis Hotel.

The fortieth President, Ronald Reagan, beat Skull and Bones Yalie, George H.W. Bush, in the 1980 Republican primary, and went on to defeat Democrat Walter Mondale in the general election that November. On March 30, 1981, two months into the Reagan presidency, John Hinckley shot attempted yet another assassination. He shot the President lodging an explosive bullet two inches from Reagan's heart

---

[3] WWW.wikipedia.org: "George Wallace."

[4] US Senate Historical Office www.senate.gov: "A History of Notable Senate Investigations prepared by the United States Senate Historical Office."

and another in the brain of his Press Secretary James Brady

The historical trend is obvious. We are in an age of assassinations and wars. Intermittently this nation has had 141 years of murder and treachery directed at our highest office. Since the Industrial Revolution, presidents and candidates have repeatedly been the targets of assassins. The social myth says that we are a Democracy, and that the peoples' will is implemented through elections. The social reality is that factions have killed our presidents and candidates for decades. On those occasions, gun-ocracy has replaced democracy. The killing and attempts to kill are intermittent. There is no need to kill when the favored candidate is elected by the dynastic power elite.

The deterioration of morality and legality in some of our institutions began when Abraham Lincoln was shot at Ford Theater.

That assassination occurred at the end of the second Civil War.

The War for Independence against England and the Tories was our first Civil War.

Our third Civil War, which our children and grandchildren will be obliged fight, lies somewhere in a future where violence against our elected leaders may well lead to ideologically centralized *coups d'etat* from local governments to the highest offices in the land.

Hollow Scene

to my relatives

If you are patient, figs will come on the trees
in Central Park, goat's milk on every corner,
loaves of bread steaming out of the Bowery
but there is no new thing under the sun—
this has happened before your cells remind you.
You will not be able to calculate this.
Is this a time to be born? Surely a time to die.
A time to refrain from embracing,
time taken from taking for granted;
a time to rend, to make masks for strangers;
a time to cast away and to cast away again;
a time to keep silent and a time to wail, to
hang from windows and bang pots in unison.
Look in the mirror when the mist parts
to see if a beast looks back at you
or a faded purple mimeo of God.
We come from dust and return to dust—
on every surface, filling up our lungs.
Remember these days of darkness, but do not
let them take up residence in your heart—
when you wake from this, whenever that may be
the mayor's irascible voice will greet you
you will meet a short man on the sidewalk
with the head of a white dog who will berate you
the pigeons will speak in broken English
all your heroes will have deliquesced
The Tombs will be open for business 24-7
the Staten Island Ferry will still run on time
and the earth will be flat, again. Far
Rockaway will be too far. I can't tell you
what your next stop will be. Just take it.

Sam and Janet Evening

Bob Dylan opened his throat and a catcall
erupted. Medulla oblongata. You'd better
switch your sward to a bass trombone
or marry your sister to a corn plaster
master of none, miniseries to all
was the verdict of the anklebiters
Terazzo Sinatra the destination
when we sailed into Hoboken harbor
she'd leopard drops on her pantyhose
leftover from our annual folderol
your letter was better than my letter
as the tomcat tried to answer the phone
indicating we were headed for disaster
three miles offshore we hit a fatal squall
the crew stood on deck flicking their lighters
and the quartet slipped into syncopation
my only thought—our tryst in the grape arbor
left there, in the rain, without any clothes.

"Something There Is That Doesn't Love a Wall"

A round of fentanyl martinis, boys,
with your smorgasbord of inedibles,
with your philosophy of animosity—
I'll raise you one and call your bluff.
Here's to greed and that maverick avarice,
Here's to dealing and double dealing—
Let's have a bilateral relationship,
Let's run the numbers, change the climate.
The news of the day, fake and otherwise:
The Crown Prince disremembers
the journalist he dismembered
ignorant of smoking intelligence
built on the paper-thin skulls
of starved Yemeni infants
after he'd hammered together
illegal settlements in our left ventricles.
Our first time together, my intercessor—
Let's secure the border and dump
systemic negative emotions pronto.
 A dozen billion peckercheckers
follow us on facebook skype and twitter—
But hold that thought—Mr. Cohen's loafers
have apparently filled with his own urine.
And what of Mr. Pecker, pecking in the wings?

Alone Among Mermaids

Through ice and cold and snow
Into the tropical sanctum
Of their indoor
Archipelago, one
By one they arrive
Unbidden—until after many

Laps, after touching
And pushing off without pause
Without rest from the sheer
Underwater reef wall,
I'm surrounded, overtaken
By a dozen
And more leaping in, flutter
Kicking almost
Naked, aggressive,

Scattered, elliptical, delicate
Architecture of kneecaps
Irresistible a birthmark
Pattern of freckles on a thigh
Shoulder blade
Cleft of buttocks and painted
Toes in swift glide
Thrusting in tandem so
Deeply focused, so far beyond
The casual solitudes, so
Deeply alone even one
Sharing my lane
Less than an arm's length
From caresses
Of my underwater imaginings—

Surely another glance
And I might perish, my flesh
Strewn among the rocks.

Night on the National Mall

The only sound's a bleared
stream of headlights
like running
water I almost can't hear moving
in and out of earshot
across an immense
span of lawn between the Capitol
dome and a towering
spike ringed by fifty limp flags—
no sound downwind
of that limp circle except
an underwater hush
now magnified by the weight
of acres of darkening marble,
as if dusk's sealing me inside
the feeling of a tomb.

Shade trees pool
their shadows too deep, brimming
with threats of imagined danger
where lamps have burned out
along the gravel
walkway, the crunch
and release underfoot loud
as gnawing insects.

Powdery phalanx of Japan's
gift of the cherry trees
along the pewter-tinted
waters of the tidal basin,
now deserted as I drift
through the festival's
pastel-scented blossoms,
each cluster delicate, soft
as the skin of newborn's wrist—
moving away from Jefferson—tall,
aristocratic on his pedestal,
lips pressed too tight,
stance a little too
jaunty, his face perhaps
a touch smug as he
stares in perpetuity

across the once-fecund pools,
his shrine lit from within
like the eye of giant
national security camera.

Everyone, by turns, shooting
photos rapid as machine-
gun fire of the same thing:
war memorials, one's
polished granite
etched scrolls itemizing
names of the dead, while
another tries to capture the posture
of an uncle who was shot and bled
flag-red; my grandfather's perfect
bronzed combat boots, fellow soldiers
in perpetual march with boot-
falls that never touch down
suspended in mid-stride, mocked
by a paver's intermittent
crawl of ants.

Still, I might walk toward an eternal
flame, cross a bridge into lush
rolling green hills planted with flawless
white crosses; witness the painstaking
ritual and stoicism of tight-
jawed sentinels changing guard; and
later, kneel as inside a temple,
drawn by the moonlit glow
of Lincoln's cragged and warty
face, left hand curled at the knuckles,
his right upturned in a gesture
of national supplication,
melancholy eyes transfixed
by the soft webbed skid of a pair
of mallards landing in unison
on placid night waters, silent
rippling slivers of current, a peace
that passes all understanding forever
trailing, closing in their wakes.

Memorial Day

A flag hangs limp
Uninspired from its pole

Steam rises straight up from the brick chimney
Of a hospital's power plant

Dissolving into blue sky
The way grief

Finally leaves the body

Because the budding tips of pines
Are holding out their new green

And every baby born to someone you know
That you have ever touched

Has extraordinarily perfect
Tiny feet and toes

After Reading Proust

I could never
bear to be inside
a second
story window,
mid-morning's
smear of light
thick as honey
across fresh
mown grass, in
a room at my desk,
writing

amid the peak
pastel blush
of hardwoods,
anemone
and bluebells
replicated
in profusion
across loamy
swales
of river bottom,

intermittent
flourishes
of wild leeks;
and lilacs,
the lilacs in full
bloom along
the garden shed—

promising I might,
in today's sudden
heat, after last night's
soaking rain, stumble
upon morels, just
birthed on south
facing slopes,
near dead elms,
in new moss,
under prickly ash.

It's still agony
at times not
to walk out from this
interior shade
into the moist
art of wildflowers
and warblers'
soft ricochet
above a sweep
of river current;

though now, half
way downstream
from when I began
this life, the river
of my body has molded
itself into an eddy,
an eddy effortlessly
circling back;
from which more
often than not I'm
content to peer out
at the same scene
from the same room,
as strangely enamored
as those first
bees I saw
four times yesterday

in the boulevard
grass (twice
in the morning
walking my daughter
to school and twice
in the afternoon
walking her home)

that with so many other
sources of nectar
to choose
instead
spent all day
mining
down
through
a shaft
the sweet
inside the dark
of a discarded
soda can.

Lust in the Heart for Rose the Dog and Jimmy Carter

Don't wander the produce aisles
Jimmy, during Indian summer when you'll
be tempted to examine too many smooth
browned arms and legs during this last
week of sundresses, or linger
too long in the scent
suspended over bins
of McIntosh – and you might
try going to the grocery store
in sweaty blaze
orange and hunting boots trailing
mud across the fresh polish, your hands
and cheeks etched by blackberry
bramble. But Jimmy, I'm somehow
saved by glancing back at my
Lab girlfriend's sad
devoted eyes through the driver's
side window, and by the nagging
worry that someone might
pry the truck door open

or smash the glass and take her
away while my eye
wanders from leeks and ripe tomatoes
and lingers too long as I fill
my wife's list. Nevertheless,
I'm saved by Rose
as she watches me grow
smaller across the parking lot
and vanish through automatic
doors, as she waits with raised
and expectant eyelashes, a peculiar
tilt and crinkle to her forehead, worried
or certain, Jimmy, I'm never coming back.

Menstrual Love

Well after check
out time, deep
into their affair,
the fugitive
lovers are fucking
on a four poster
in a posh hotel:
She's on top
when her hand
moves to prop
another pillow
under his head,
leaving a perfect
handprint
of blood, whorled
lines he eyes
with amazement,
while kissing
the coppery
decoupage
that's bloomed
across her chest
and neck; and later,
as they shower,
mesmerized
by the volume
of watery blood

flowing from
his inner thighs,
transfixed
by her pose
of pained serenity,
her vulnerable
yet languid
inward gaze
as hot spray
thrums her back,
an image arises
of arrows piercing
San Sebastian's
female torso,
along with the spear
thrust and churned
into Christ's side,
and finally of a rag
soaked in vinegar
stuffed
into each other's
thirsting mouths.
While she strips
the bloodied sheets,
he slides bloody
cases off pillows,
and together
they hurriedly roll
these with the ream
of white sanguinary
towels they'd used
to wipe themselves
into a big ball
outside the bathroom
door; a mound
he eyes carrying
their suitcases
past as though
a dead child were
wrapped inside.

Countdown

Sometimes the line between civilization and chaos seems so weak!
As if for one long moment that might last indefinitely
Strip mall parking lots are nearly full,
With steady lines at fast-food drive-thrus,
And everyone going about his or her business
In a manner that's neither more nor less functional
Than it usually is, and seems will always be so,
But for a white cop who presses his knee into a black man's neck,
Grinding his face into the pavement until he can't breathe.
By nightfall, the city's on fire, a police precinct torched,
Protesters smashing windows, looting, Molotov
Cocktails, curfews, National Guard troops in riot gear,
An angry mob that won't disperse despite pepper spray,
Billy clubs, rubber bullets, tear gas, flash grenades.

Sometimes the line between civilization and catastrophe seems so thin!
As if we're always mere seconds away from a passenger
Jet flying into a tower of the World Trade Center,
Shatter and burst of the initial fireball—what was that?
Jet fuel's thunderous black smoke, melting steel, human beings
Trapped above deciding whether to jump or burn.
Or an interstate bridge about to collapse
During rush hour in Minneapolis,
A condominium in Miami
That crushes half its occupants,
The next Three Mile Island
Or Chernobyl.

If only the line between civilization and chaos weren't so thin!
I might hold out more hope, I might put more faith in technology,
Engineers, elevators, automobiles, satellites, fiber optic cable—
All the appliances and gadgets that make life easier.
I might not shudder when filament of an incandescent
Light bulb suddenly flickers and pops,
I might worship the miracle of the Smart Phone in my hand,
That I can connect with anyone, anywhere in the world,
Summon an infinite web of information, news,
Knowledge, ideas, essays, great works of art—
But it's useless without an outlet, a charger
Cord as its battery dwindles and conks out.

And sometimes a symbol of civilization explodes so unexpectedly!
I remember the faces of my classmates,
How faces in the crowd gathered to witness the launch—
Happy, smiling, cheerful, beaming—
Like one mask of the theatre
As we all chant in unison the thrilling
Countdown Five! Four! Three! Two! One!
That lifts the space shuttle off its pad—
I remember how all our faces drop
At once into a tragic frown
As Challenger hurtling forever
Heavenward yet already flaming
Too much like a comet
Suddenly bursts—
How the blast plumes outward
Then hangs suspended as it molts
Raised and jointed pinchers
From its triangular head
Into an evil-looking praying mantis,
Protean as it swiftly morphs
Into a monstrous science fiction
Creature yearning to die in the sea,
Giant cephalopod, squid, octopus,
Finally a lifeless slowly falling jellyfish
While the CNN camera follows a single
Limp tenacle spewing earthward
Gravity's suction cup of white smoke—
Our teacher after switching off the special live broadcast
Turns around to face us
With a pained grimace, distraught, her grief
Stricken face a silent stream of tears.

If only the line between civilization and oblivion weren't so thin!
I might be optimistic, even as one country invades another,
Bombs its civilians, maternity wards, children's hospitals.
I might be optimistic if there was ever a weapon, a gun,
Big or small, primitive as a spear, complex as a missile,
That we ever made, that we have not used.
A trigger is designed to be pulled,
A fateful button, secret codes
Someone's desperate, vengeful,
Or indifferent finger will eventually punch.

Congress

From across the aisle they glare
In contempt of each other's enviable girth,
Another grudge match is set to begin,
Flab rippling as one-half of the body
Politic slaps its belly against the other,
Grunting, huffing, yawping barbarously.
When the goal is to be immovable,
Being fattest is to one's advantage.
While inside this circular chamber
The whole point is to fight for position,
Snouts down at the public trough,
In order to grow so obese
That they don't get pushed
Out of the ring by their opponent.
When lobbyists arrive promising
A secret, high-calorie diet of private,
Corporate slops to the highest bidder,
They all squeal in unison
With voracious delight.
At their biggest match of the year,
On Election Day in America, only
By their red and blue silk ~~mawashi~~
Diapers can you still tell them apart.

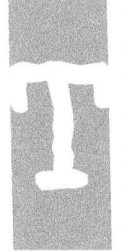he buses all looked the same in the dark. Kevin squinted through the snow at the open belly door, like a dragon's stomach, where the others had piled their gear to be stowed. That girl with the insane pompom hat—what was her name? she was everywhere—darted through the crowd and climbed onto the bus. This must be the one.

He dropped his snowboard, boots, and duffle bag at the edge of the pile—oh, he had to piss, there were bathrooms on the bus, right?—and, fumbling for his pack, he moved towards the door. His foot pawed the air. He grabbed the handrail and tried again. Good. Just wasted enough. Leaving Colorado at dusk, by morning he'd be halfway to Nashville, back to Vandy, well not back to Vandy as it turned out, but back to … something.

Grabbing the seat tops, Kevin wobbled toward the back. He dropped his pack on an empty seat and made his way to the bathroom. The watery light made everything greenish, oh this ride was going to be brutal, and then, relieved, he wobbled up the aisle, searching for the reflective tape on his pack.

The bus filled. Hopefully, Jason would show up soon and snag the seat next to him. Kevin settled in and closed his eyes.

It didn't matter. Nothing mattered, really. This was the Zen state he'd been aiming for. After complaining about school for the past year—how Vanderbilt was full of privileged snotty nobs, how he had no idea what he wanted to study, so why was he in school anyway?—his tuition waiver had been revoked for something he never could have predicted: his mother, an anesthesiologist on the teaching faculty, had been intervened on—packed off to rehab for prescription drugs, and while she was "on leave," his tuition waiver did not apply. His *mother*. His beige, uptight mother. Of course, he'd seen her unhinged, mainly at him. His DUI last year had been a real tearfest, but he couldn't get over his mother getting in trouble, getting caught.

Everything blew up before Christmas. He'd already paid for the Ski Club trip, so they let him go, but without the tuition break, his father didn't want to pay for a semester at Vanderbilt, and since Kevin wasn't enrolled, he couldn't live in the dorm, so everything unraveled pretty damn quickly. His mother was in rehab for three months. Minimum. Three fucking months. He hadn't visited yet, and his older sister, usually his ally, had been blunt on Christmas Eve.

"You know, the whole troubled teen thing really stressed them. Don't you think you're done playing that card? Don't you think you've been an asshole long enough?"

Harsh. He swirled eggnog in a tumbler. Breakfast, dessert, and alcohol all in one viscous package; the opacity was kind of gross. Thinking of it now made him queasy. He pressed his coat against the window and went to sleep.

*

He woke in the dark, thirsty, and pulled out his phone. 6:43 a.m. Shit. A text from Jason: *Where r u?* Kevin sat up, looked around, but couldn't see him. He closed his eyes. Oh, he needed water. Next to him, a guy in a navy parka stirred, half-opened a crusty eye, and looked out.

"Where are we?" Kevin asked.

"Nebraska. It's always Nebraska."

His accent sounded Russian, but Kevin couldn't tell if it was real or a joke. "Funny dude."

"The American tundra."

Kevin tried to picture a map of the United States. A hot fear started in his stomach and moved towards his bowels. He sat up, straighter, and looked around the bus. No one looked familiar. Tingling waves ran out to the rest of his body, and he remembered the night he'd gotten his DUI, the glare of the police station, the molten shame that he'd done something he couldn't take back. Across the aisle, a girl wore a purple sweatshirt. Winona State. He smirked. It wasn't spelled right. A row ahead, and on the other side, someone else wore a purple sweatshirt. Could he have gotten on the wrong bus? Oh, not possible.

*

Later in the morning, after they had stopped for gas and started up again, after he had subtly confirmed for himself that yes, he was on the wrong bus, and no, Winona was not spelled Wynona, like Judd or Ryder, that he was going to somewhere else, he had to ask his seatmate.

"Hey, where exactly is Winona State?"

The boy looked at him without expression, turning up one corner of his mouth. "You got on the wrong bus?"

"Yeah, but I don't want them to drop me off in the middle of nowhere, so don't say anything, okay?"

"Where were you going back to?"

"Tennessee. Nashville."

The boy snorted. He put his head against the seat in front of him, wheezing with suppressed laughter. When he sat up, he smiled and wiped his eyes.

"Idiot. When I came to this country, my father and I landed at the Minneapolis airport, got a taxi, and my father said, 'Take us to the Russian neighborhood in Minneapolis.' The driver looked at us like we were crazy. He said, 'There is no Russian neighborhood. Where do you want to go?'"

Kevin sat back. "So, I'm screwed, but really, where are we going?"

"Minnesota."

"Shit."

"Not really. I come from Siberia. You want to talk shit? That's some shit."

Outside, miles of corn stubble poked through the snow. He had maybe twenty-five dollars left. No credit card. What could he do? Call his dad and ask for a plane ticket? It seemed ridiculous, even for him.

He'd always imagined that, after he was done screwing up, his parents would be there, waiting for him. When he got his head together, it would seem as if he'd come through a passage, that he'd still be himself, but he'd join the world of people who knew what they were doing.

After the DUI, his mother insisted he go see a therapist. It became a condition of living in the dorm, rather than at home, and he figured he could bullshit his way through fifty minutes a week if it bought him a little freedom. It reminded him of being a kid, when he'd had to see the school counselor because his mom had put him on drugs for ADD, or ADHD, or whatever they were calling it then.

This time, the therapist, Mark Something, was a nice guy, low-key, but Kevin didn't feel like talking. He sounded witless, even to himself. He tried to play the accident down, but it had scared him. He'd crashed into a STOP sign, flattened it, and as he told this to the therapist, the irony of it was too much.

Mark tapped a pencil on his pad.

"What was your father's response?"

"My mother's the one who's so damn overwrought."

"That may be true, but I'm curious: how did he react?"

"He barely reacts to anything. He's an engineer at heart. He works at 3M. My mom's like a spastic whippet. If you made her stand still, she'd screw herself into the ground. And my dad basically pacifies her by agreeing with her. Sometimes I wish he'd man up and put his foot down, or get pissed off, but he pretty much goes along."

"Do you think you're trying to provoke a reaction from him?"

"Jeezus. No." Kevin picked up a small ceramic elephant resting on a table near his chair; the figure was handmade, kind of impressionistic. "I just wish he'd just tell my mother to take a breath. She's constantly vigilant, Mad-eye Mooney, you know?"

The therapist drew his eyebrows together. "I don't get the reference."

Kevin set the elephant down. "He was a character in those Harry Potter books. His motto was 'Constant Vigilance!' That's my mother. She's exhausting."

*

The bus changed gears and slowed, a twenty-minute stop for food and coffee. What could he do? He couldn't afford a hotel. He could ask his seatmate about crashing at his place, but Boris, or whatever his name was, didn't seem too friendly.

The gas station smelled like old hotdogs; the coffee would be terrible, so he ordered hot chocolate. When he turned around, the pompom girl, her red pompom flattened, was behind him. She ordered a cup of tea.

"Hey," Kevin said.

"Hi."

"If I tell you a secret, you promise you won't bust me?"

She had a round face, wind-burned cheeks. She seemed like the kind of person you could trust to babysit.

"Sure, why not?"

"I got on the wrong bus. I was supposed to be going back to Nashville, but instead I'm going … I don't know … wherever this bus is going."

She giggled. "Seriously?"

"Yeah. Is there a hostel, or any place that's cheap to stay in Winona?"

"No, I don't think so."

It frightened him, how quickly she answered.

They walked over to the counter for milk and sugar, and she chose a wooden stick to stir her tea. "Are you a jerk or an ax-murderer or something?"

"No. Well, maybe a jerk sometimes, but not on purpose."

"What kind of jerkdom?"

He wondered where he should draw the line. "Well, I've changed my major at least three times in two years, I don't always remember to put the toilet seat down, I'm kind of unconscious about my surroundings…"

"Obviously."

He smiled. He felt ridiculous standing there, hoping his presence might invite help.

"My housemates are gone over the break, and one of them has a brother who's staying in her room for a week. You could crash on our couch for a few days, but if you eat my groceries, or you're weird, he'll hurt you. He's actually very sweet, but he's one of those Crossfit guys. He could beat the crap out of you without even trying."

Kevin took a deep breath. "No one will need to keep me line, but I'd really appreciate the couch. What's your name?"

"Tabitha."

He took a sip of hot chocolate. "Cool name."

"My mother liked the show *Bewitched*."

Kevin mentally scrolled through images from *Nick at Night*. "The show where the woman wiggles her nose to get stuff done?"

"That's it."

"You're named for someone with magical powers."

Tabitha nodded towards the door. "We should get back on. This'll be our last stop. I'll look for you when we get off."

*

When they got off the bus and collected their luggage, it was morning, but the day felt fuzzy and distended. They lugged their gear to a boxy house near campus. In the living room, she pointed to a brown, corduroy-covered couch. "That's you," she said. A short man with a bushy beard emerged, looking as if he'd just gotten out of the shower. His crumpled ears were small; his biceps filled his shirt sleeves. He nodded to Kevin, who stretched out on the sofa, used his coat as a blanket, and went to sleep.

*

When he woke, it was afternoon, and he lay still, trying to think of what to do. He didn't want to call his dad, who'd probably say: *get a job, work your way home.* Kevin called Melissa.

"Hey, 'sup?"

"Sup? Snowboarding made you all gangsta now?"

"Hardly"

"How was the trip?"

"Well, it's not quite over."

Melissa waited.

"I got on the wrong bus coming home."

"What? Where are you?"

"Minnesota."

Melissa snorted.

"I seem to be providing a lot of amusement for people. But yeah, I'm here in the frozen north, and I'm broke. A girl is letting me crash on her couch—but I've got to get cash to get home. I haven't called Dad yet."

"It won't do you much good. He went to Puerto Rico."

"What?"

"Apparently, he and Mom made plans months ago, and he's been to see her a few times, and she told him he might as well go."

"Jeez."

"I was kind of worried about him with Mom gone, and when I called him, he said he'd decided to get away. Apparently, he needs to do some thinking."

"Did he say that?"

"Not exactly, but that was what he implied. Anyway, good luck reaching him—he's not exactly responsive. And I don't have a couple hundred dollars to spare."

Kevin picked at a bare spot on the couch. "What's it like … seeing Mom?"

"It's weird. You have to be on a list to get in."

"Exclusive."

"No, you have to be approved so that people don't put their dealers on the list."

"Damn."

"I know. I guess the whole addiction thing with anesthetists and anesthesiologists is tricky. They basically have to do super rehab. And I talked to Dad after you left—Mom'll be pissing in a cup until she retires—and that's the best-case scenario. They can prosecute her. Each thing she's taken could be a separate charge. Can you imagine Mom in jail?"

Both of them were silent. His mother always left a gleaming kitchen before she maneuvered her Saab out of the garage. A peace settled on the house when she was gone.

"We're like a flashback in *Orange is the New Black,*" Kevin said.

Melissa hiccupped; he'd gone too far.

"Poor Mom, is she having a hard time?"

"Of course! She has to deal with all the stuff she's been trying not to think about."

The world pressing in. He knew the feeling. "Well, I'll try to sell my snowboard and my boots. Seriously though, can I hit you up for food money? I can't mooch off this girl who's letting me stay at her place."

"Text me and I'll figure something out."

"Thanks, Melly." He set down his phone.

Outside, the afternoon light deepened, becoming granular. His stomach gnawed. He needed a shower. In the bathroom, she'd set out a towel with a note: *Here—* . Funny girl.

After a shower, he felt better. He dressed, slipped his computer into his pack, and stepped outside.

Wind riffled at his neck. He pulled his hat over damp hair. The cold wasn't too bad. Tabitha had pointed in the direction of downtown: over the railroad tracks and towards the river. A spindly kid stood at the crosswalk.

"Food & coffee? Wi-fi?" Kevin asked.

"Acoustic Café. It's a few blocks down there." The kid pointed with an oversized glove.

When Kevin walked in the door, the smell of deli sandwiches hit him like a wave. He ordered coffee and a turkey sub with everything on it. The cafe had heavy dark furniture, windows that looked onto the street, and clumsy artwork on the walls. While the cashier rang up his sandwich, he studied a poster: *Frozen River Film Festival.* February. Hopefully, he wouldn't still be here. The cashier gave him a number, and he settled into a booth.

Kevin flipped open his laptop. Was this town big enough for Craigslist? Probably not. Maybe someplace in town would buy used equipment.

He searched for flights to Nashville, but they were expensive. Even if he found a job, he'd have to work for almost a month to buy a ticket. And a shuttle to the Minneapolis airport cost $50. He punched in *Greyhound,* but when he tried Winona and Nashville, the options wouldn't load. A girl with curly red hair brought his sandwich, and he pushed his computer aside. The bread was soft and warm, and the sandwich, with some kind of dressing and yellow banana peppers, was amazing. Online, he searched for used equipment stores, sports stores, pawn shops, any place that might buy his gear.

He drank his coffee and debated buying another sandwich, but he needed to save money for tomorrow; he picked up the last bits of lettuce and dressing, then headed out to the street.

Second-hand stores, gift shops, a law office, a bank with ornate stained-glass windows, an acupuncturist, outdoor store, no, it was the pawn shop. He pushed open the door. Guns & DVDs. Camo jackets and fishing poles. He walked up to the counter where two guys talking to each other ignored him.

By the cash register, a stuffed squirrel, a real one, perched on its hind legs grabbing its little squirrel balls; its tiny mouth was open. Kevin snorted.

"Yeah?" A guy in a feed cap looked over at him.

"Do you guys take snowboards, boots, stuff like that?"

"Not really, no."

Kevin walked out into the street. He passed a yarn store, a hairdresser, a veterinary clinic. He turned a corner: Adventure Ski & Cycle. When he pushed open the door, the smell of new tires washed over him. At the counter, a guy with a huge brown beard peered over his glasses at his phone.

"Do you buy used equipment?"

"We buy used bikes, that's about it."

"No used snowboards, boots, that kind of thing?"

"No, we rent skis though."

Back outside, it was getting dark.

*

The next day, he headed in the opposite direction. He passed a store called Sole Sports, but it had high-end gear; they wouldn't buy used stuff. He passed a credit union, industrial buildings, a used clothing store, then saw a sign: Winona Food Shelf. He stopped in the cold. He

could just go in, see what they had. As he stood, watching his breath plume in the air, a woman parked a beat-out Chrysler in front; she helped a kid out of a car seat in back while an older kid, in a thin coat, climbed out by herself. No, no way, he'd be embarrassed to go in when other people needed it more.

He walked for what felt like miles. At the end of the bus ride the other day, he'd seen a Target, a Walgreens, and other box stores; he wondered if they were hiring. How much was minimum wage here? He calculated what he could raise by selling his gear and how much he'd make by working. He didn't want Tabitha's roommates to come back and be pissed that he was crashing there. Finally, he came to the edge of a parking lot: Walmart, Target, a place called Fleet Farm. In Target, he asked if they were hiring.

"In a few weeks. You can fill out an application online."

He tried Walmart, a fitness store, a liquor store. Clearly, this was the wrong time to look for work. Hibernation mode, no one was hiring.

He'd always had money from lifeguarding in the summer and selling the Adderall he'd stopped using. Selling the Addy was pocket change, really, but he'd never needed much. His stomach knotted in on itself. He saw a McDonald's across the highway, but even that wasn't cheap. The sky was growing deep gray, and snippets of conversation swirled around him: *looks like snow, yep, it's coming.*

He went back into Target and walked to the grocery section. He pretended to shop while he looked around for stockers. He unzipped his coat a little and, standing in front of the granola bars, he waited for some girls to roll their cart into the next aisle. Glancing in both directions, he grabbed a box and stuffed it in his coat.

Moving down the aisle, he felt for the top of the box. He ripped the tab, pulled out a granola bar, palmed it, and walked over toward Electronics. He pretended to study the headphones while he opened the wrapper. Fake strawberry. He ate four bars, walked over to Sporting Goods, pulled the last two bars out of the box, then quickly stuffed the empty box behind a display of yoga mats. Feeling a little sick, he went outside for air.

*

Dark and wind blew off the lake. He hoped he could get back to Tabitha's. He was heading in the right direction, but all the tiny houses looked the same. He texted Tabitha to get her address, and luckily, he wasn't too far off. He felt as if he'd walked all day.

The smell of spaghetti sauce greeted him when he opened the door.

"Hi there," Tabitha called from the kitchen.

"Hey."

"Want some spaghetti?"

"That'd be great."

Tabitha swirled a little water in the jar to get the last bit of sauce, then dumped it into the saucepan.

"You want any help?"

"Nah"

"Didn't have much luck selling my gear."

Tabitha puckered her lips. "Did you try that bike & ski place in town?"

"Yeah."

"There's a Stuff for Sale in Winona Facebook page. I've never tried it, but friends of mine have bought stuff off it."

"I'll try it." He didn't want to say he'd asked about jobs, because he didn't want her to think she'd be stuck with him. He flipped open his computer and got on Facebook: Stuff for Sale in Winona. He went into the living room, snapped a picture of his boots and board, and loaded them onto the page.

"So, what do people do for work around here?"

Tabitha served up mounds of spaghetti, and they sat down at the kitchen table. She twirled spaghetti on her fork and considered.

"Work-study at the university, I don't know. Kwik Trip, tend bar, work at the food coop."

"I've got to figure out a gig where I can get quick cash."

"There's factory work around here, but I think you have to go through an agency."

"How bad does the snow get here?"

"Sometimes we get a lot." She pushed her plate to the side and half-closed her eyes. "I'm gonna crash early. I still feel like I'm jet-lagged from not sleeping on the bus."

"Yeah, me too." He wanted to lie down, put his feet up, but knew the next move. "I'll do the dishes. I really appreciate the pasta."

She hesitated.

"Really, I'll wash up and just leave stuff on the rack."

"Cool." And Tabitha smiled and headed upstairs.

He squirted soap into the sink and filled it with warm water. He'd never washed dishes at a restaurant before, but how hard could it be? Did places want an online application, even for that? He thought about Acoustic Cafe. The sandwiches were amazing. Maybe he could try there tomorrow. He finished the dishes, folded the dishtowel on the counter, lay down on the couch to finish making his Facebook post, and fell asleep.

*

He spent the following days asking about jobs at any place it seemed possible to get hired. Everyone was hiring "in a few weeks." The veterinary office downtown would consider having him walk dogs or clean out cages, but they wanted references, and he didn't know how to reach his manager from his lifeguard job.

The incoming storm made him feel trapped, but people seemed inspired by the idea of snow: he sold his boots and board off the Facebook ad. He made arrangements to meet the guy at Tabitha's, then went to the cafe.

He ordered a huge hoagie, claimed a spot at a table, and connected to Wi-Fi.

He googled Amtrak and punched in Winona and Nashville.

Bingo. From Winona, he could take a train to Chicago, arrive in the afternoon, and an 11 p.m. bus could take him to Nashville. $147 student rate. He figured in his head: he'd gotten $120 for the boots and board, and he'd just bought a huge sandwich; he still needed at least $40.

When he got up to put his basket back, he looked over the counter at the guy prepping sandwiches.

"Hey, do you know if they're hiring here—dishwashing, mop-up work? I'm broke and I need a gig."

The boy looked up. "I don't know, but you can ask." He pointed to a woman on the phone.

The woman had a ponytail and a headband, like a college kid; she hung up, wrote something down, fielded Kevin's question about work, then plucked at a pair of brightly colored glasses hanging around her neck.

"Nothing here," she said, "but I've got three rental properties and the students are still away. We'll get snow tonight, so I'd pay you to do those. Two of them are on corner lots, so you have to do both sides."

"I'm on it," he said. "Just tell me where to go."

"Do you have a car?"

He shook his head.

"They're not too far apart. Listen, I've got to finish some things here. Why don't you come in tomorrow morning, and I'll give you the addresses and point you in the right direction. There's shovel in the garage at each place."

"That'd be great. Hey, would you throw a few sandwiches into the deal?"

"Sure," she said. "No problem."

*

Snow started to fall as he walked back to Tabitha's. The town seemed peaceful; like an exhale, the snow was starting. Inside, Tabitha sat on the couch with a friend, the friend texting, her face hidden by a curtain of brown hair.

"What's up?" Tabitha asked.

"Got some food, got work shoveling snow tomorrow."

"Industrious."

"Gotta be."

"This is Vickie."

Vickie glanced up, "Hi."

"How'd you get work shoveling snow?"

"Boyish charm."

Tabitha smirked.

"A manager at Acoustic Café said she had some rental places."

"Nice."

"Yeah. Got sandwiches too. And I meant to ask before: how does a little town like this have a film festival?"

Vickie touched her phone and looked up. "The university hosts it—students can go for free. Last year, the best movie was about the gay rodeo. 'Queens and Cowboys.'"

"What?"

She turned to Tabitha, "And Carl was in it—."

"What are you talking about?"

"Didn't you see it? Carl, my orientation teacher, had a part in it."

"No!"

"Yes! There's this whole gay rodeo circuit and someone made a movie about it."

"That's so cool!" Tabitha said.

*

When Kevin woke the next day, snow glimmered on the branches, on the mailboxes, everywhere. The world was serene. He needed coffee. He dressed and headed over to the café. Almost six inches of snow had fallen; people were shoveling already.

When he walked into the café, he ordered a tall cup of coffee and two muffins. A girl started to ring them up, and he looked for the manager, who nodded and told the girl she'd take care of it. She handed him a piece of paper with three addresses and a sketched map.

"Shoveling is serious business here." Kevin bit into a blueberry muffin.

"It's a legal thing. If someone slips outside your house because you haven't shoveled, you're paying his medical bills."

"Damn," he said. "I better get going."

*

Nashville occasionally got a storm that whitened things up, but he'd never shoveled snow like this before. He got a rhythm pretty quickly; the sidewalks were mostly even, and the snow was light where it hadn't been packed by walking. He thought about the film festival. It'd be fun to go, but he had to get back and see his mom; he didn't really want to visit her, but she'd be relieved to see him, and he owed her that, at least.

When he'd finished the last walk on his list, he looked around. A few houses still had snowy walks—maybe other people would pay for shoveling.

At the first house, no one was home. At the second, a hungover-looking student squinted at him, and Kevin could tell the guy had no money. At the next house, a little bungalow, an old woman in a red cardigan came to the door. She didn't seem to understand his question.

"Never mind, hey, would you like me to shovel your walk? Just for free?"

"Oh, young man, that would be very nice." She crossed her arms and patted her own sweater sleeves; her knuckles were huge, her fingers angled almost like flippers.

He shoveled her path and the sidewalk in front of her house. She waved to him from the window.

He felt good. Better than he had in a long time.

At the next house, an angry-looking bald guy opened the door. "My snow blower is busted. And I just paid to have it fixed! I usually do Mrs. Donovan's walk for her."

"Does she live over there? I just took care of it."

"Did you charge her?"

"No, sir." Kevin couldn't think of the last time he'd said 'sir.'

"Good man. I'll pay you twenty-five bucks to do my walk and sidewalk and driveway."

Kevin looked at the driveway. It wasn't long, but it wasn't short either.

"Okay."

*

The kids next door came tumbling out in snowsuits and boots and hats—they looked ready to tackle the Klondike.

"Hey, Mister, shovel it over here so we can make a fort!"

Mister. Wow. Kevin started pitching the driveway snow in their direction. They laughed and waved their arms. A little boy, waddling like a penguin, started wailing. "My mitten! Where's my mitten?"

His older brother laughed. "You don't need it."

"I need it for snowballs!"

Kevin felt a guilty start—had he covered it up with snow? He walked over to their yard.

"Dude, don't get worked up, I bet it's here." He used his shovel to pull away a clump of snow, and there was a blue mitten. Genius.

The kid held out his arms, Frankenstein-like. Both cuffs had clips to keep mittens attached, but one clip was open, filled with snow. Kevin had forgotten about those things. When he was little, he'd always lose his hats and gloves, which pissed his mother off. He had these mitten clips, or whatever they were called, but at a certain point he refused to wear them. That winter, almost every day, his mother sent him off to school with a hat and gloves, and he'd come home without either. Kevin slapped the snowy mitten against his leg, cleared the snow out of the clip, and clamped it onto the mitten. He worked the mitten onto the kid's hand.

"There you go!"

The kid smiled, shyly, then reached for a clump of snow, aiming at him and grinning.

*

By the end of the day, Kevin had shoveled a bunch of walks, returned the shovel to the house he'd taken it from, and collected two sandwiches from Acoustic Cafe along with his money. He went back to Tabitha's to tell her he'd raised enough for a ticket home.

*

The following morning, waiting at the railroad station, he wondered what it would be like to stay in a place completely by accident. If he hadn't had equipment to sell, he'd be stuck. Tabitha had saved his butt, but he was merely a funny story she'd tell on future ski trips.

Since he had to change in Chicago, he'd texted a friend from high school, Ezra, who lived there. It would be good to see him—even for a few hours between the train and the bus. Kevin hiked his pack onto his shoulder. He tried not to think about visiting his mom.

As the train left town, the tracks dipped low, close to the river. The Mississippi, wide and gray, glazed with ice, had backwaters broken up by sandbars and small, forested islands. On the far side, the bluffs stood stark and mountainous. Melissa would like this; she'd majored in geology and worked with water conservation or reclamation or something. He realized it was stupid that he didn't actually know what she did.

When they were kids, they used to goof around with a Canon *Powershot* he'd gotten for his birthday. He'd make little movies and edit them on his computer. Melissa was willing if not imaginative. He constructed scenes that didn't rely on her talking, and sometimes, he'd set up a visual joke she wasn't aware of until she saw the movie herself. He liked choosing music that didn't fit too neatly—that was one of his peeves: obvious sad music in the sad place, scary music to signal tension, it was dumb—music should work by juxtaposition rather than illustration. He liked to play with fades and transitions. Even his parents had liked those little movies. His dad would put his hand on Kevin's shoulder, lean over his laptop and say, "Play it again."

*

When he stepped onto the platform in Chicago, the smell of diesel smoke and fried food was like a shot of adrenaline. A text from Ezra:

Meet me at the Art Institute
Where?
So. Michigan Ave. 1-mile down Wabash
K

Chicago felt like a real city. Nashville, so imbued with its own sense of itself, felt provincial, like a large small town. The wanting and competitiveness among all the aspiring musicians and songwriters bled into the air, and of course Vanderbilt had its own traditions and history. He'd like to live somewhere without the past constantly in his face.

The Chicago Art Institute announced itself with banners and broad stone steps. Clumps of people stood in the somber afternoon, and Kevin scanned the sidewalk before recognizing Ezra, whose uncombed hair was longer now. With a scraggly beard, skinny jeans, and black Chuck Taylors, he was an urban version of his high school self. His arm draped over the shoulders of a girl with crimson hair; they studied something she held in her hand. Kevin called his name, and Ezra looked up.

"Hey, you made it," Ezra said. "Kevin, this is Rhonda."

Spiders crawled through her ruby-tinted hair. Kevin squinted. Bobby pins with little fake spiders on top.

"Nice spiders."

She grinned. "Let's go in. I'm freezing."

"Can we get coffee?" Kevin asked.

"Yeah, there's a place inside," Ezra said.

They started up the steps.

"So, did you really get on the wrong bus?"

"Yeah."

Ezra smiled out of the side of his mouth.

"I lucked out—this girl let me crash on her couch."

Inside, Ezra led them towards coffee. The museum was light and airy, filled with people, and Kevin felt cheered, as if he was somehow getting back on track.

"So, you're not going back to school this semester?" Ezra sipped his coffee and grimaced.

"Naah. I lost my ride. My mom's in rehab, so I don't get a tuition waiver."

"No shit. Your mom?"

"Yeah, that's what we've all been saying."

"Sorry, man."

"It sucks, for her I mean, and that's partly why I've got to get back. I think having a visitor—even me—might help."

"Some rehabs are nicer than others," Rhonda said. "Rehabs for doctors are posh."

"It's been kind of … startling. I'm supposed to be the fuck-up." He grinned, half-expecting to be contradicted, but Rhonda simply waited for him to continue. "But it gives me a break. I mean, it made sense to go to Vandy while it was free, but I want to get out of there."

"What are you studying?" Ezra asked.

"Nothing. I've got no idea. I'd love to go to film school— not to be a big director, just to know how to do some of that stuff—but my parents would flip out."

"Columbia College has a film program," Rhonda said.

"Here in Chicago?"

"Yeah, it's got all kinds of stuff. Book Arts, Writing, Film…" Rhonda slapped the table. "Half my friends go there. C'mon, I want to see the Frank photos."

"Seriously, again?" Ezra had become the personification of languid.

"What's the exhibit?" Kevin asked.

"Robert Frank's *The Americans*."

"Photographs. They're brilliant," Rhonda said. "He took them during the '50s—he was on a Guggenheim and police officers in the South thought he was a vagrant. Jack Kerouac wrote the introduction to the book."

Ezra smiled as if indulging a child. "They really are pretty good," he said.

*

The black and white photographs had a velvet darkness. Kevin lingered in front of one photo: "Trolley New Orleans—1954." The white faces in front, pruny and disapproving, the black faces in back, a buxom woman in her Sunday coat. A little white girl sat in front of a sorrowful-looking black man. A wavy chiaroscuro filled the top windows of the bus. Kevin thought how satisfying it would be to capture something like this, to frame what others didn't recognize and make them see it.

*

Outside the museum, Ezra, smelling of cigarettes and patchouli, slung an arm around Kevin's neck. "Y'all come back now, you hear?"

"I just might." Kevin grinned.

*

On the bus back to Nashville, Kevin dozed in the throb of oncoming headlights. Maybe he should move here, get a job, see what he could do. His dad was always asking, *What's your game plan?* as if somehow, overnight, Kevin would wake up and have one. Occasionally, his father would say that Kevin could get a job in the warehouse at 3M, as if this was a job for a dolt who didn't go to school, but maybe he could actually do that for a couple months. If he worked full time between now and maybe April, he'd make bank. His mother would be out by then.

When he got off the bus, he spent his last few dollars on a uber home. Inside, the house felt vacant. The refrigerator was empty. He texted Mel.

Home

You'll see Mom, right?

Tomorrow

You have to let them know you're coming. She put you on the list.

Glad I made the cut.

Good luck.

His dad had left him his mother's car keys and the address of the clinic. It felt strange to get in a car with complicated temperature controls and leather seats. The clinic was on the other side of the city, a little outside of town, and the road curved past sparse forest and large homes. His hands twitched as he pulled into the parking lot. The building was modern brick and glass, like a hospital, but the plants out front, faux domestic touches, seemed like a bad disguise.

He had to be buzzed in. A woman at the desk said his mother would be out.

Everything was pastel and chrome, windows and soft light.

When his mother came through the door, she looked smaller, diminished. No jewelry, no make-up. Her blonde hair was gray. It was strange to see her without the armor of perfection.

"Hi Mom." He hugged her awkwardly, aware of his height. She smelled like a familiar soap or shampoo, and the normalcy comforted him. "You lead the way. Where can we talk?"

"The cafeteria."

He must have raised an eyebrow.

"Open space, so we can't have anyone bring drugs in."

He followed her, a half step behind, down a mauve hallway with bright artwork, into a room with round tables. A few other people were grouped at tables around the room. A pitcher of water and paper cups sat in the middle of a table, and she poured each of them a cup. He sat down next to her.

"I should have brought you a real cup of coffee."

"You wouldn't be allowed to bring anything in."

"Oh." It felt strange to be at a loss for words. So many times he'd wished she would just be quiet, but talking was all there was now. "This might sound weird, but what do you *do* all day?"

She twisted her mouth. "We have NA meetings, physical therapy, individual therapy. Group. Yoga. We have to exercise. Guest speakers. We stay pretty busy."

He started to ask if there was anything good about it, then realized what a stupid question that would be.

"You start to realize how much of your life was centered around your addiction. It's been…" she spread her hand out onto the table, then looked away. She shook her head.

The scent of fabric softener wafted by him. He tried to brush it away.

"I don't think your life was centered around that, it was around work and teaching—and us––."

Her smile was wan. "No, I'm afraid it was about hiding, about making everything look right, and trying to smooth the way for you and Melissa, which was folly, of course." Her face crumpled like a dead flower. "I haven't been a good mother."

"Mom, how I am is not your fault."

She sniffed. "Not completely. But I didn't help. It sounds silly, but I really didn't know how controlling … oh, it's embarrassing, this recovery jargon … how controlling I really was." Her lips wobbled, and she took a sip of water. "I thought I knew best about … well, everything." And then she started to cry.

He moved his chair closer and put his arm around her. Her shoulder blades felt bony under his arm.

"I shouldn't have given you medicine as a kid. I should have let you run around more." She gasped. "We should have sent you to a school that lets kids bounce on yoga balls … or lie on the floor, or …"

His pulse pounded in his head. He tried to take a deep breath. No one seemed to notice his mother's tears, but he wished she would stop.

"Mom, I hate to tell you this, but after a certain point, I didn't take anything. All that time you thought I taking stuff, I was flushing it."

She stopped crying for a moment, sat up and looked at him. Her gray eyes were teary, but assessing; recalibration, clouded by doubt, moved across her face.

"Really?"

"Yeah, really." He knew this wasn't the time to mention how much Adderall he'd sold or given away over the years.

She turned away and started to cry again, silently.

"It's okay." He took her hand. "It's okay." He knew it wasn't but didn't know what else to say. When she had stopped crying, and wiped her eyes and blew her nose, he began again. "I don't know if you'll think this is funny or not—" and as he opened his mouth, he realized maybe he shouldn't tell her how wasted he'd been. "I got on the wrong bus in Colorado and ended up going back to Minnesota instead of Nashville."

"Minnesota? How did you get home?"

"I ended up in this town called Winona, and I sold my boots and snowboard, and shoveled a bunch of walks to make money. I took the train to Chicago and a bus back to Nashville. So, who knew? You can get from Minnesota to Nashville for cheap."

He described his Russian seatmate's amusement at his predicament, and seeing Ezra in Chicago, and Rhonda's creepy but interesting bobby pins, and his mother laughed at his descriptions, blinking through her tears.

"So, Mom, I'm thinking about something—."

Her face made an inquiring mask, as if trying to stifle her first reaction.

"I'm thinking about moving to Chicago."

"What would you do there?"

"I don't know. Live for a while. Do a job and save up some money. Columbia College has a film program. You know, production stuff. You make movies as part of your coursework. It could be interesting."

She put her hand on his arm. "Sweetheart, anything that makes you feel optimistic, that's what you should do."

"I'm going to ask Dad if I could get a gig in shipping or the warehouse for a few months. I'd save up some money, and I wouldn't leave while you were still in here."

"That's very sweet." She tried to smile. "They really want us to come out of here changed." She looked at him directly. "I can't imagine going back right now, everyone knowing."

He'd assumed she'd do anything to get out; her capitulation frightened him. "Well ... people are going to know. They'll just have to get used to it."

"None of this is anything like what I thought it would be."

"I think that's how everything is," Kevin said.

*

When they said goodbye, he hugged her for a long time and kissed the top of her head. He wondered if the gray had come on quickly, or if she'd just stopped dyeing it.

"Thank you so much for coming, sweetheart."

"Sorry it took me so long to get back here." It felt strange to stand there, not knowing how to say goodbye. "I know this is supposed to be some big self-examination time, but you know, we're all just doing the best we can."

Her lips trembled. A teary smile seemed the bravest expression she could muster.

*

Out in the parking lot, he started her car. January in Nashville was muddy and dank. He thought about Chicago's smoky buzz and Winona's crisp air. He'd liked shoveling snow, feeling the warmth inside his clothes while the air was cool. He thought of the old lady whose walk he'd shoveled, the way she'd watched him from her window, as if it didn't surprise her that random people might take care of her.

He stopped at the end of the driveway. To the left, the road bent sharply. Across the street, a convex mirror, mounted on a tree, let drivers see oncoming traffic. He remembered being small, his mother holding his mittened hand, teaching him to look both ways before crossing the street. Cautiously, he pulled forward, his eyes on the mirror, making sure that no one was coming, making sure the road was clear.

Snow Upon Stones

It's snowing and I've gone to the woods, over muted frozen loam for no other purpose than to gaze upon its transformation – to the abandoned quarry, what remains of it. Now only the occasional fox labors in the crevices. Ninety years ago, rough fellows cut and hauled these stones, each girth more than a man, and at the end, the cliffs played out, scattered them like pebbles dropped from a careless palm. I don't recognize these faceted planes as their green moss trousers are dusted with white, a crazy Cubist landscape better than Braque.

"Whatchalookinat?" The cross-country coach happens upon me and thinks I'm odd – clearly dumbfounded. While I remain polite, still distracted by snow upon stone, my joints growing stiff in the cold, he drones on over his many dilemmas, the infuriating details of his new home, the disposition of pipes, wires, cabinets and carpeting, switches and faucets – chaos, the myriad creatures of his making – *maya* run amok. He's got the latest watch under his sleeve which performs all manner of astonishing tasks. He gazes at it three times while doing all the talking, and points at it: tap, tap, tap. And he's got noise, the latest political blather, stuffed reciting in his ears, a plethora of opinion, analysis, and prediction. Doesn't he apprehend? Chuang Tzu would kindly tutor him: while the tyrant and the borders of his dominion are eventually obscured, the poet's regard of the ephemeral, gazing at what's in front of him, will more likely endure.

Patron Saint

Also a professor, on his feast day,
I recall my obscure patron, Saint
Cassian of Imola, the schoolmaster.
Apparently, a nasty old bastard,
His students, every boy, loathed him.
An obstinate, myopic parishioner,
He was condemned to death
For refusing to offer sacrifices
To the pagan Roman gods
As decreed by Emperor Julian the
Apostate, that perfidious backslider.
(Didn't Constantine settle all this –
His mom being baptized and all?)
Though Cassian's martyrdom
Was gruesome (Most all martyrdoms
Were ghastly. That was the point.)
And though it was rather inventive –
Somewhat, perversely entertaining –
He preferred to be, more traditionally,
Stoned, flayed, immolated or crucified.
His pupils bound him to a stake
And, weary of Homer, stabbed him
To death with their iron *styli*, scribing
Flesh instead of classics in wax tablets.
The saint's object lesson for me
Is something unintended but apposite.
It is not so much inspiring as practical
And has nothing to do with which god
Is which in a theological hierarchy.
Simply, compassion, a little empathy,
Is more useful than obedience.

Laughing Buddha

On the little oxbow shelf
Along Old Woman Creek,
A bend I frequent now and then,
There's a quiet, contemplative spot,
Lush foliage and silent decay,
Where I considered placing
A statue of the laughing Buddha,
One of those concrete casts,
Yard art found on the corner
Of two country highways.
I'd paint it a bright pink,
Proof of my whimsy —
Oh gee, spontaneous me.
The idol would remind me of
Suffering, three of four *Noble Truths*,
The elusiveness of nirvana,
The futile pursuit of absolutes.
Obviously, the object would declare
That I was here and put it there.
Or maybe an image of the Virgin Mary
Or Saint Francis of Assisi would do
Popular icons on tidy suburban lawns.
(A little-known martyr would express
My hip penchant for obscurity.
Better yet, how about Uncle Wayne or
Mrs. Hennel, my second-grade teacher?)
If it were Mary, I would enjoy
A perceptible increase in mercy
And a marked decline in despondency.
If Francis, I wouldn't meditate upon
Saint or pope. I'd recall Assisi,
Those exquisite Giotto frescos
In the basilica's upper chapel,
The toy-like architecture, the charming
Characters in dramatic tableaux.
Or I'd pine for that *trattoria* discovered
Around the corner from the Roman temple,
The pasta superb, surpassing the usual
Tourist fare and worth the climb
Up steep, uneven medieval alleys.
On second thought, any effigy
Remains out of the question.

Gerald Lynch

Free Love, At a Price

t was twenty years ago (today) that Alcohol Al Rubin, still intermittently sober at the time, sponsored my application for residence in the government-subsidized housing project, *the* Project. At the time I was renting (by the week, yes) a mouldy single room in the basement of a decrepit clapboard on Sandy Hill's Mariposa Street. Had the plenitude of silverfish, centipedes, sow bugs and cockroaches been contributing their fair share to the rent, I'd have been able to continue solvently. As it was, moving into the Project was a step up both the residential and economic ladders (rent and utilities were paid). I then continued slovenly, but as things turned out the move proved to be a step down life's stairway to hell.

I'd met Alcohol Al at the Hibou Jam, our local, where the two of us often closed the place drunk as funky skunks, and about as popular, especially on, say, Tuesdays and Wednesdays, when staff are eager to get home and dream their compromised American dream of life in a detached Canadian house. Mid-week is *the* bitch of a time for losers in dead-end jobs, eh? But never mind that. Instead return with me now to that first hooking-up with Alcohol Al …

The bar having emptied over the course of the evening, Al and I, still strangers to each other, were knocking about, nodding agreeably at our own pale reflections over the fuming urinals, beginning to acknowledge each other.

On about the sixth side-by-side he spoke: "Ah, my es-steaming friend!" He had a low voice, which resonated in that chamber.

Shaking off I said, "If these are urinals, why aren't the toilets called arsenals?"

He hooted. Perfect. Said, "I know I've 'sploded there!"

Our isolated tables slid closer together in socializing overture, if yet leaving an exit gap where the spills and weepings of beer could drain. We were always pissed and railing at the staff about the same kinds of drunkard things—government spending, immigration, the world generally going to hell—topping each other as we called back and forth across the gap like gay shepherds.

I'd just shouted at the retreating back of one of the exhausted waitresses, because she'd not even tried to hide her sneering contempt when I'd answered once again that, no, I was not yet done with *that*. I'd called, "The Prime Minister's wife's a sushi-eater too!" Though not so loudly as to get me thrown out, which the bartender was always raring to do, especially mid-week, particularly to me.

I had immediately begun playing bongos on my table-top and singing, "I been told when a boy kiss a girl …"

The waitress knew my name, but all she'd said in turning away was, "Screw you, Ringo."

I'd then been gentle in my homophobic retort because I knew Ringo had to be at least 5'7" on his Beatle heels. (Such calculations are not inconsiderable in the socializing of a 5'5" man.) And I was secretly impressed that such a young woman had recognized old bad Beatles.

At the adjacent table, the room otherwise emptied, Al said with dismissive exaggeration, brushing the idea away with a backhand, "Waz a little illicit love?"

"Wha …?"

Bowing deeply, he did an answering roll on his own bongo table and ended with his mouth going *pah*: "I hear they're using a secret room in the Peace Tower to soak tax-refund cheques in an estrogen potion—turns bitches into Stepford Wives!"

I fluted back, "Won't work, wives don't get to touch the refund cheques!"

Ignoring my point, he declaimed, "I'm gonna get me one of those cheques for Summer."

"Why summer?"

"*Summer*: name of my lady love, wife, and bestest friend in the *whole* wide world." He showed just how big the world was, then placed his right hand over his heart, signaling irony as loudly as canned laughter.

"*You're* married?" I blurted.

He acknowledged the insulting implication with tight lips. "In a manner of fucking." Then hooted again what had already become his Alcohol Al hoot, hardly a laugh at all, just more weird irony.

Henceforth I was there for Al, if primarily there for the beer. But a close second for the company of another such devoted drinker, who soon emerged as a model member of the class *ebrius mortuus*. I was attracted too by Al's obvious erudition. I assumed the source of the attraction was mutual, as I'm pretty sure he didn't have anything untoward in mind when we first cozied up in the Hibou Jam that night and got evicted together. At least nothing sexually illicit in mind at the beginning of our … well, yes, our friendship. Regardless, early on I tested him with my hypnosis parlour trick.

"My friend, have you ever been hypnotized?"

The abruptness of the question evoked his deeply cringing face. "What? No. I'm pretty sure I couldn't be hypnotized."

"Everyone says that. Would you be willing to try a little scientific experiment that can quickly be done here and now?"

"I'm game."

"You have to be totally susceptible, that's key."

"Sure, why not?" distractedly hoisting and wagging the empty pitcher. The exasperated waitress took it away.

The table momentarily empty but for half-empty glasses, I hurried.

"Relax, Al. And look at me. *Salt*. Imagine the sharp taste of salt on your tongue."

"Got it, salt." He wasn't really trying, and if he'd not been expecting the return of a full pitcher, he'd have not tried at all. But it didn't matter, as long as he continued cooperative.

"Look here then. Imagine a saltshaker. Visualize that I'm holding a glass saltshaker with a silver top. *See* the perforations, the grains adhering." I mimed holding the shaker close to his face. "Can you *see* it?"

He was irritated having to give his attention. "I see it already. *Visualize*, my hairy ass."

"Good. Now take the saltshaker from me." He played along and held the imaginary saltshaker in circled thumb and forefinger at his breastbone.

"This part's important, Al. Raise the saltshaker above your mouth, all the time *thinking salt, salt, salt*. Now, tip that saltshaker upside-down and shake some *salt* into your mouth. You *will* actually taste salt. *You will*," I intoned for effect in the bullshit mesmerizing.

He did so, shaking away, even vigorously. "Shake it, Al! Shake that saltshaker!"

The bartender looked over, raised his eyebrows, then smiled (a rarity for me or Al).

Al stopped. "Sorry, new friend, but I taste nothing. I told you I couldn't be hypnotized."

"Al, you're not being fair to the experiment or to me. *Concentrate* on the reality of the saltshaker, the bitter taste of salt on your tongue. Try again, please, and give it hell. You *will* taste it."

Good man, he did us told. The waitress returned with our replenished pitcher (I believe the Hibou Jam didn't wash them for the likes of us regulars). Seeing burly Al with his head tilted back at an angle, his mouth open and tongue protruding, and jerking away at his phantom shaker, she spurted first then said, "Hey, big guy, practicing for the weekend? I didn't know you two were of that persuasion!" She plunked down the pitcher and turned away.

Al froze with hand in mid-jerk. His eyes widened; he got the picture. He'd barely shouted his "You fucking faggot!" before starting to laugh at himself. Having scarcely been able to restrain myself, I was relieved to join in a homosocial howl.

So he'd passed my test.

You may not know so, but dedicated drunkards of our voluminous capacity and achievements will overlook much else in the character of a drinking companion for the simple companionship in drinking. Along with which socializing, two drunks are much better than one at finding more drink when the bar closes, especially when one of them holds his booze better than the other, as did Al, and has a home only a short walk away, and always a few brew in residence, and a tolerant wife named Summer.

Nor will such a boon drinking companion ever mention food. I don't know what it is biologically or psychologically with me, but at the second pitcher—the second being my gateway drug—whether I'm starving beforehand or not, food stinks. All I can think of is more beer. Not even sex, which is a joke to a drinker of scope. But never food especially. If I'm into the beer and enter a space where food is cooking, I can vomit right there on the threshold. If we make it inside and some amateur drinker's considerate partner offers— having poorly concealed her surprise at my presence and slurred demand for a beer—

"We *do* have some Beau Lugnut that would go with the Cornish hen," which from the parking lot I had smelled cooking in its red-brown clay pot of fowl oozings, I might just throw up right on her and get me to hell out of there pronto. I mean no disrespect. It's a reflexive thing with me, organic, hormonal, psychosocial—whatever explanation for unacceptable behaviour might turn your empathetic crank for a drunk such as I.

So I was always reassured when, should a sojourning drinker suggest food in Alcohol Al's presence, he would make a face of hemorrhoidal irritation and squirm in his seat and look around for the waitress. An agreeable soul though, Al; if pressed, he would tolerate the interruption of

continuous suds to his gob. First though, reluctant Al would attempt to tempt our visitor with an item from the Hibou Jam's menu, say one of those nuked chip-and-cheese confections, or some insanity called "buffalo wings" that, being all bone and gristle, may well have been the rare truth-in-advertising. If unavoidable, agreeable Al would go to a restaurant, and once there even nibble a thing or two. But inside of an hour, miraculously we'd be back at "our table" at the Jam with Al removing half the whole pitcher of beer from his big happy face or pouring for me with a heavenly smile as from a Cana cornucopia. Half non-compos-mentis, I would then be in the only reliable heaven drunks know here on earth.

Playing catch-up at our table in the Hibou Jam one evening, I broke every unspoken rule by saying abruptly, "Al, is your life really this meaningless?"

(I'd just overheard some punk on the bus say that I was suing the city for building the sidewalks too close to my ass.)

Al startled, then roared (he was a great roarer too, was Alcohol Al), "Meaningless? *Really*? It's all here, buddy!" Spreading his arms like come-to-Jesus.

No one ever came, because no other regular ever visited our table. Not the fat old whore with diminishing portfolio. Nor the shrinking old man who knew to sit near the exit, overdue for his weekly shave and monthly welfare cheque, who appeared to be living on whatever sappy nutrition resides in toothpicks and the yellow skin fringing his fingernails, and who apparently believed that staring blankly into emptiness made him invisible to the powers. Periodically, on his way to the can Al would pour such nodding geezers a glass, emptying the suds from our pitcher before setting it meaningfully on the bar. When I once tried to mention this charity to Al, he made a warning-off face. At heart a good guy, humble Al, forever, amen.

I folded my hands in my lap, though he'd set before me a refilled golden chalice. "I'm serious, Al. Look at us. How can we continue so meaninglessly?"

He dropped the big grin and smiled gently. This rare Authentic Al was like the living room of an abandoned house when a dirty shard falls from a window and a little light gets in. But you're still worried about the floor joists, and you wonder how and why you're again in this place.

Al was doing his tight-mouthed grim grinning, nodding weak agreement just to keep the game friendly.

He snapped his head to the right. "Man I just love being out of it!"

He hooted, ignored his shapely draft glass and hoisted the whole pitcher to his big mouth, as was his wont when he'd had enough of talk.

I mark that moment as the beginning of the end of all bonhomie pretence between me and Alcohol Al. From then on we just drank our miserable beer and argued intensely about nothing and everything. Turned out the only real thing we had in common was being out of it and arguing about nothing.

But I should qualify that "rare Authentic Al" above. I'd already observed that Al was quite the actor, quite the dramatizer. It could well be—I now believe it so, come to think of it—that Alcohol Al was the closest thing to an Authentic Al.

Al eventually told me about his life in the Project and how I could apply successfully for residency. He knew members of the Project Board, the Superintendent, and tricks for jumping the queue (chronic health, victim of sexual abuse, Native ancestry, refugee, and various other victim positions; I drew the line at "reformed sex worker," though I admire that designation, which I wouldn't at all mind having on my tombstone, just not applied while I'm still living).

I always brushed him off saying I was fine where I was.

But Al persisted uncharacteristically. He brought a Project application to the Hibou Jam, and I—or he rather—filled it out on a neighbouring dry table. In the identification section at the top of the form, he'd given my given name and surname correctly, but for my middle initial had scrawled "Tekhahawonahhwithha." As far as I know, no authority blinked at this. Who would dare?

The upshot was that I moved into a "bachelor apartment" on the second floor of the Project, a room so dank it could have served for a mushroom grow-op. On the pretext that I was undergoing sexual reassignment (he never told *me* that one!), Al got some LBGTQ charitable outfit to furnish the place quite generously, complete with state-of-the-art TV, a 65" plasma curved-screen wonder.

I began spending time in Al's unit next door.

But speaking of second stories, I must turn now to Summer Rubin.

Despite Al's ironically calling her "Lady Love" and all those chivalric things, Summer Rubin really was all of them, and more, much more. Al's speaking so only revealed that, despite her pearly value, she meant little to that ironic swine. Al was an alcoholic, recall, and all an alcoholic cares about is alcohol: circumventing all obstacles to it, getting it, drinking it, getting more of it. Repeat. The Four Horsemen of the Apocalypse have topped the Mount of Olives? I need another beer. Behind them comes Jesus in sunburst. Could you dim it down, puh-lease? Daddy's got a headache.

But yes: Summer Rubin.

Easily the loveliest, the sexiest, the most attractive, the most beautiful woman I've ever met. In keeping with her name, she only ever wore breezy flower-print sun dresses with thin shoulder straps done up in a small white bow on each tanned shoulder, and little else. That is (so you don't miss it), *she wore little else.* One, at least such a one as I, could not be proximate to such a one as Summer Rubin without acute consciousness of plentiful firm flesh moving behind the translucent dress that swung on her like a joyful bell. *To* put too fine a point on it: she never wore a bra and would often forgo apparent underwear.

Even in the dead of winter, Summer Rubin's forehead always shone with a glistening film of sweat.

Al may have held his booze like a camel holds water, but he just about always went immediately to bed not long after returning home. Abandoned so, Summer and I were shy at first alone with each other. I think because she was a 5'8" knockout and I was … well. Nevertheless, regularly left alone we soon sorted out a friendship, one more realistically predicated than Al's and mine. And despite what you may understandably have understood from my waxing hornily above, the absolute absence of sexual tension had a lot to do with it.

I should clarify: we all drank, but Summer was never drunk, though as a point of honour she was never quite sober either. She had this charming quirk where she never opened a bottle for herself; instead, she would sip from Al's and mine (not at the Hibou Jam, mind, but at the Rubins' when I'd visit of an afternoon, either on the way to the Jam or post-Jam). That was the first thing about her that put the fluttering heart across me, her uncapping our bottles and taking two big swigs per round, then her growing giddiness. And I loved her (thank you, Beatles).

Greater truth to tell, I was madly in love by the end of our very first meeting, after I'd helped her help Al to bed, and we shared the night's ultimate beer. We were talking about basketball because she played power forward on a pick-up team of old high school friends.

"Ever play, Nigel?"

Drunk as I was, I'd been growing increasingly anxious as she talked of her elbow-work under the basket. I worried about my sweating as she watched me sweat, her pale blue eyes as non-judgmental as a basset's. She bragged delightfully of catching some "pipsqueak" of a skinny redhead on the temple that very day and knocking her stone cold. But I sweated more profusely, worried that the dizzying effort at restraint would cause me to tip sideways onto her kitchen floor. Unable to hold it in I outed myself:

"I'm quite short, you know."

"Oh," she sang, glancing away as if someone had called distantly. And returning her attention: "No, I meant … I'd not noticed, but I guess you are short, for basketball, I mean. Still," she continued, alarming me as she reached across the steel-trimmed corner of the Formica table and emplaced her right palm over my heart, "you're well proportioned, though, slim and well-muscled, especially through the chest." She placed her left hand on my back and actually palpated my girth. "I *have* noticed, and I bet other girls have too."

I was hardly there anymore; it was as if some demon musician were playing my head four different ways like a squeezebox.

"I'd have made a good jockey, eh?"

"Maybe, don't knock it. But I was thinking more an Olympic gymnast."

You were?

She wasn't smiling. She brought her rare bottle to her mouth, sipped, then rested its ridged neck on her wet lower lip, just gazing pleasantly across it at me from eyes pale blue as after-rain skies.

It was at least as much the beer, I think, though it could have been the usual—my feet finding no sure purchase on the floor—but as she withdrew the bottle I did fall from my chair and was saved from total collapse only by the wedging wall.

Summer tossed her head and trilled. Then seriously, touching back a silky blond strand: "You have a bruised heart, Nigel, badly crunched and crushed, I can feel these things. If I met the girl who did that to you, I'd punch out her lights."

"You can tell all that, Summer?"

The way she looked at me, I could tell she could tell.

"Another thing: you're funny in a way that always includes yourself, uh, *sarcastic*. I'm sure that's why Al likes you so much. Do you have any idea how that sense of humour affects women? I mean, real women, not the humourless fem-amazons hunting for an alpha male guaranteed to crush *their* hearts, that way proving the unjust power of 'the patriarchy.'"

"I've not really known that many women, Summer, what they want."

"This woman then."

No awkwardness saying that miraculous thing either!

Clearly not seriously I said, "I think I'm in love, Summer."

She removed the bottle from her plump lips in a kissing sound.

I *was* in love again, ever wanting to, what was I to do, couldn't help it.

That became our routine: put sopping soporific Al to bed, then split a one-for-the-hallway last beer as we performed on our own late-night talk show. And what didn't we talk about under such influences?

She was of course an out-of-joint flower child from the resurgent 1990s. Al was an older eighties refugee in rejection of that me-decade. They were supposed to have been living off the land, which they had tried for five long years somewhere in the Gatineau Hills, but … But who cares about such bio-details from our late-night tête-à-têtes when proximate I was drawing up my nose and into my mind essence only of soap-and-lightly-perspiring Summer?

At some point in their unimportant past Al had been told that his home brew, or more likely the quantities of it he'd consumed, had destroyed his stomach, some of his tract, and had turned his liver into something like grotesque *foie gras*. He was given a government disability pension and reduced to imbibing light draft. Then to living in the Project. And that's enough about Al. His path to nothing was right before his eyes.

Summer's stepfather had sexually abused her. "No penetration," she hurried, her qualifying hand like a sudden blossom on my foreshortened forearm like a dog bone.

"Still …," said judgmental Nigel.

"I don't think he could help himself, Nigel, it was compulsion disorder … like alcoholism, I guess. A disease really. Pat loved me, I'm sure of that. When I turned sixteen, he swam out into the lake and never came back."

I must have been looking uber-judgmental. She half-opened her mouth fish-wise. Then said, "He just came on my leg, Nigel." She glanced toward the doorless bedroom where Al, sprawled on the floor mattress, was arguing loudly in his sleep with a mud-hole-snorkeling hippo.

Normally confessional culture sickens me, but not so with Summer Rubin. She was different. We were. (Aren't we all when it's *our* adulterous crime or amorous 'emotional affair'?) She was always hopping her chair that much closer to our shared corner of the kitchen table. Even that was different: no woman had ever moved closer to me. And such a beautiful woman doing so? Mother Mary Herself may as well have appeared on the fridge door and announced that God the Father had sent her with the good news: *Hephaestus says the femur extensions are good to go*!

"On your leg?" My good-listener echo technique.

"Well, high on my thigh."

"Top or inside?"

Insensitively I'd gone too far. She dropped her chin and was sniffling. Her straw-coloured hair was parted down the middle, exposing a white line most vulnerable. It attracted powerfully, that blond-hedged pathway, promising passage to a sunny field where children and near-midgets frolic for Mother Earth's pleasure. I struggled to restrain my hand from her head, from planting my lips in the hairy divide.

Suddenly Summer's confession of wintry trauma fired me with rage, a raking prickling heat. Forget echoing Narcissus, I was uncontrollably (okay, drunkenly) enraged:

"If I met your father right now, I'd punch out *his* lights!"

"Stepfather, Nigel," she said into her lap with curious calm. "My father died of an overdose when I was fourteen."

"If I met the man, I'd kick the living shit out of him!"

Her streaked face came up, she smiled small, like the sun chasing rain from a field:

"Pat died for love of me. People can't help themselves, Nigel."

"The dead. Death: the last refuge of the criminally sick."

She snorted and laughed. "I like the living shit better. Me and you and Al—the living shit!"

Wit too from this beautiful woman, and in such a psycho-emotional clinch? I was impressed.

It was a relief to join her laughter. But it got out of control, and we ended crying in each other's arms, all bonding tears and snot. It was an awkward parting that night. She remained dead-panned at the table, and I let myself out. I was worried that she'd resent me for witnessing her meltdown. But there was no awkwardness when next I showed up drunk with Al for more beer.

Nor was it only such intimate revelations over the night's ultimate beer that bonded us. After she found out I was a graduate English student (at the time I was in my eighth and final year of a two-year MA program), we often talked about books and writers. Summer, a ferocious reader, loved two writers especially, named Alice Munro and William Trevor, a Canadian and an Irishman.

"They *are* very good," I said woozily, only ever having heard of Munro, who had won something like the Toronto Book Award.

But I had never read a word of either. My field of expertise had been Renaissance Drama (and boy did I love dropping that impressive bundle on the idly curious). Not my formal studies for the MA, which, being all coursework, didn't require a thesis. RenDra was my RA work, my Research Assistantship, which was drawn out over four years, and which just managed to support me in the way graduate students become accustomed to. Which is to say, scarcely, something just below Maldivian mosque mouse. And not really the whole of Renaissance Drama but restricted to examining the compulsive records of one OCD-candidate named James Halliwell-Phillipps respecting early seventeenth-century productions of the well-known Shakespeare classic, *Titus Andronicus*. That was the scholarly obsession of the chubby beardo Full Professor, Dr. Fallon, who would make this madness his life's work (and a comfortable life he got out of it too, thank you Mr. and Mrs. Taxpayer). At least the material was all online, if by the bursting cloudful. The point is, just as I was about to be kicked out of the program I completed the course-only MA without ever having taken a literature course post-1800.

As a result, educated I had hardly read anyone who'd written in the past few centuries (it was such fun—and so easy!—to fake it when Hibou Jam visitors, having sussed my education, asked me about *their* favourite writers: Stephen King, J.K. Rowling, George-a-bunch-of-Rs Martin, Naomi Campbell, that guy who wrote the screenplay for *Lord of the Rings*, and such). Till that 'Summer time' the only contemporary writer I'd ever read and enjoyed was Kurt Vonnegut Jr., because Junior's gently pissed off humour complemented what I'd liked in Stephen Leacock (my only other most favourite writer, from a first-year Canadian literature course I'd been forced to take). It was Alcohol Al, another surprising avid reader, had pressed Vonnegut on me. Summer did not like Vonnegut: *too* sarcastic.

Summer claimed for Trevor and Munro, "They're so good at showing what a dark force love can be."

"Yes," quoth Nigel (not *yeah* but *yes*), "but that's not all, is it?" Oh, I knew how to fish.

"No, not all, I didn't mean to imply that, but black romance especially. They show the horror of love."

"Great horror stories," glossed Nigel gone an echo too far.

"What?"

Thank God she frowningly left it at that.

There was lots after that though. In fact, if I could tell a story straight, I'd have put our book-club chat before the revelation of paternal molestation, because that was the sequence of events. But that's the way regular love stories unfold for normal healthy people: we have spiritual affinities, what a coincidence! I've had personal troubles in my life! Fancy that, so have I! Our love was written in the stars! Agreed. Let's fuck—not as others do but as foreordained lovers.

That was *not* the way things progressed for me and Summer. We really were … *different*.

A body can confess her/his darkest secret only once, truly and impressively, even if subsequently s/he may continue to trade off it (which Summer never did, I hasten to say). But it took book talk, our biblio-therapy, to draw us together and then cement an intimate relationship.

On the pretence that I needed reacquaintance, I borrowed a few of her two favourite authors' books. That increased my library to four favourites, and it took Mr. Leacock a long while to work his way back to the top of the short list. Love is like that. We will jettison anyone and everyone, anything and everything, first principles, preferred tastes, friends and relatives—all disposable in the primary drive to reproduce our genes under cover of starry-eyed love. We are—all of us, from Adam to Madam—such shills for the God of Propagation (a.k.a. Nature) as nightmares are made on. In this my love story (my shoulda-known-better), the only good news remaindered was that the Leaky Steamcock (as his students called him) and I did eventually become fast friends again, and not only because *Sunshine Sketches of a Little Town* has nothing to do with debased sex (see Munro for that) but that too.

Our Project units were nothing if not nothing. Forget swinging a cat, more than one occupant and you were always brushing one another, mainly with elbows and asses, as you moved about. Al and I took homo-panicked care, but Summer was always a free spirit.

Along with never taking a beer for herself but sipping generously from ours, another of Summer's charms was that she made sure Alcohol Al and I were continuously supplied. To wit: she kept the suds flowing. So not only every man's dream but particularly "a drunkard's dream if I ever did see one" (The Band). She would reappear in the living room always with two bottles, from each of which she would first drink two-fisted like a smacking kiss before handing them over and removing the empties. A loving service, and nothing servile about it. To whoo.

If she bowed to set Al's bottle beside him, her back to me, he kept his eyes on me, at first with that aggressive smiling frown of his, then the tight-lipped grin, *because* my face was only a foot from Summer's small beach ball of a bum, my aquiline nose in line to park in its crack. Then she'd turn and, odiferously close, set down my much-needed beer, in the act unselfconsciously hanging her incredible bra-less breasts for my appreciation—tits, I tell you, that were as fit and firm and fair as her namesake's sunny day. When I'd tear my male gaze away, it would be to find Al grinning broadly at me. He had a mad, a demented, grin, that Alcohol Al.

In the Hibou Jam, he began teasing me, right around the time of penultimate pitchers.

"She really likes you."

"And I really like Summer. You are one lucky man, Al my man."

"No, my little man, I mean *really* likes." His eyebrows rose like he was semaphoring my very worst self to come across and have a peek.

"What?" I snapped it. "And knock it off with the *little man* business."

"She says you're the *only* man who understands her, big guy; after me I mean, of course."

"Who? Me? I've never understood a woman in my life."

He held the empty pitcher above his head, looking about for the waitress, hoping to stretch last call. But they were on to us. Without turning, the bartender barked, "Tap's shut off, buddy, go home to your wives and children." And snorted derisively at the very idea of it.

"Yeah," rising Al grumbled loudly, "from my Hummer straight to the cognac and into my cigar humidor, you fucking dickhead."

"Hey, Caitlin," the bartender called to our backs, "how's the ol'"—he did the standard blowjob mime—"going?"

The filthy dishrag missed its mark and slapped the back of my neck like the devil's own kiss-off.

Over the coming weeks matters intensified.

"I wouldn't mind at all, Nigel my man. Free love has always been Summer's and my trip. We've never betrayed our principles, not like some. Besides—"

"*You are nuts*, Al."

"I'm also impotent."

I showed nothing. "What's that like, my friend?"

"Like nothing, of course. Or not *like* nothing, it *is* nothing. I think it was the wrong drugs at the wrong time."

"Well, I hear they've now got the right drugs for that condition."

"I don't do any drugs anymore, this stomach of mine. Summer deserves better, and you know that better than anyone. She's never talked about another man the way she talks about you, big guy. You'd be doing us both a favour, and yourself, take it from me, I remember …"

Jesus Christ.

Drunk (why am I even saying?), I went home with him. A silent walk on a steamy summer evening—past all the hot oily-smelling cars occupying pride of place, past the peeling sagging clapboard houses of Lowertown, past the gas station where frowning drunken dads were filling up for adventurous rides, past more swaying and stumbling belligerent losers—to our Project home.

Heart like a wiffle ball I said, "I'm shit-faced, you know."

He giggled. Al had a delightful giggle.

He shouted before his door was fully open: "Honey, we're home!" False giggle. "And we are good to go, babe!"

He bumped around, off the door jamb and into a stout pirouette, exaggerating the stumbling act.

Summer appeared—the right word for it—from the bedroom, barefoot, wearing her flimsiest sun dress, and with dandelions in her hair. Dandelions and daisies were profuse around the Project, in the scrubland, from cracks in the tarmac, and even from rifts in the brick façade of the building itself—which is where they should have remained. *What* was she up to?

As per our routine, I took Al by one of his bushy armpits and Summer crutched the other, and we steered him through the bedroom door (with extra consideration, I imagined). I turned away to the living room but couldn't help hearing the unusual, heated mumble between them. Then the usual sound of Al falling to the floor mattress—"Goodnight, sweet Al," Summer exaggerated, most unusually—and his immediate snores, this time sounding of a

cartoonish theatricality. No arguing with himself this night.

My molars tingled, but I didn't have to pee. That function had shut down and its workers wobbled off the job.

Summer reappeared. Standing by the entrance to the galley kitchen I turned and smiled: "Good old Al, eh?" I'd never said anything like that before or thought it.

She smiled with un-Summer-like tentativeness, then singsong, "Elephant in the room! You really on for this, Nigel dear?"

I was instantly slimed with sweat.

"Oh, just relax, honey. Go sit down."

I did. But *dear*? *Honey*? The unusual endearments made me feel I was on a visit to a southern whorehouse.

She brought one beer, took her tithe, handed the bottle to me, all the while doing her non-judgemental female gaze.

"Are you *sure* you're comfortable with this, Nigel?"

"Well, I, yeah, I mean, like, I'm not sure, that is, Al said you, he was like insist …"

Standing before me in the over-lit living room, she looked diaphanous, her full body draped in filigrees of light that seemed to come from everywhere. She may as well have been naked already. Apparently, we shared that thought, for she reached her left hand to her right shoulder and vice-versa, like some goddess blessing herself for a plunge, and simultaneously tugged the small white bows, and the nothing dress dropped whisperingly to the golden parquet floor. Her fair-haired crotch was fairly in my face. I was suffused with the warm aroma of fresh-baked pie.

I set down my bottle and said, "I … My god but you're beautiful, Summer."

"Stand, Nigel. I'm not just pussy."

I'd been so fixated on her mound—its pale hairs more down than pubic bush, all bowing inwards to the crease—that it and not Summer could have issued the order and self-denial.

"No? Uh, I mean, *no*. I know that, I'm sorry."

I inhaled deeply and knew to stand before I'd faint. She moved to within nipple sensory communication; on pink stippled areolas hers stood like plumping raspberries—no needling nipples for Summer. I'd never seen such generosity. She reached both hands and roughly pulled my black t-shirt over my head. At sight of my furry red torso, she herself breathed deeply (at the time I was, at a stretch, 5'2").

I dropped my underwear with my jeans, stepped out of them, and stood there cockful in my sockless runners, as soon managing the old rise-n-shine.

With her cool left hand Summer cupped my neck and gently held me to her, as with her right she held *me* as might an experienced milkmaid, warmly coaxing the muscle. I was breathing hard as the blood rushed to serve our God (His edict to our first parents) in a communicating bridge across the breach. I reached behind for her hips primarily to steady my swooning self in the unlikely event of her letting go; at my elevation, my palms propped pendant cheeks like two rubber containers four-fifths filled with honey. I was further at full tilt. I began to lose thought. It was about to happen. I would give myself—

When framed in the arrow formed by Summer's tufted left armpit Alcohol Al appeared from the bedroom and instantly refocused my vision. He was naked too, grinning his mad-Al grin, obviously wide awake. Naked but not unencumbered, for an ancient camcorder sat on his left shoulder and a power pack slung down from his right. I could suddenly have been transported to Russia, or Siberia.

Summer and I turned in our half-embrace to face him, our own "Two Virgins" pose, and we both inhaled, if differently. I glanced sideways; she was still smiling for her close-up. I don't know what face I wore. Horror? I let go of her.

"Don't stop, don't stop," pleaded Al, moving the viewfinder to his right eye. "This old girl's all powered up and good to go too."

"What!" It seemed to be my favoured response to much that Al had been saying lately.

I looked at his cock of course, which was massively flaccid, a strangely two-dimensional wide arrow, flat as a flounder, as if engorgement were more alien to it than transitioning to cunt would be. But it wasn't Al's waste of whang stopped me. It was his hairy white maleness generally, the sagging pale ass when he turned to flick the dangling power cord, the long powerful quads. Most of all though, the hairless alabaster legs of an old man (what age *was* Al?) insisted that I take senatorial sober second thought.

What the hell was I doing?

My jockeys and jeans were up in answer, my tumescence as soon de-.

"Hey," laughed Al falsely, dollying in for *my* first close-up, "when's a dwarf like you gonna get another shot at a woman like Summer? And c'mon, babe, you'd agreed to the whole deal."

Summer had dropped into the armchair, her knees clapped shut, her bunched dress bundled to her chest and mouth, like she would stifle the crying for as long as she could.

I found it in myself to place a hand on her head. She looked up at me with flushed and tear-streaked face; I smiled as warmly as I ever have and said, "Never, of course. Sorry Summer."

I pulled on my black t-shirt, slipped into my runners, and fled. Al's mad laughter chased me along the hallway to my door: "Who do you think you are, Withers? *I'll* tell you who, you fucking dwarf …"

Oh no you won't, Alcohol Al. I'll tell *you* who I am, you and anyone else who'll listen, or no one will. In the very first place: I am *not* a dwarf.

But through our walls and Al's roaring Summer's increasing crying came clearly, climaxing in wailing before subsiding. Hard on its tapering tail rose a raucous murder of Lowertown's monstrous crows tuning up the morning's crepuscular sky (who'd ever have thought morning could be so like evening?). Looking out my back window into the day's grey dawning, I found myself sober as a crow.

Ars Poetica

I'm a madman in a grease stained jumper
Removing bolts I can't replace. It's time
For my dead motor to come out
Of my old skid steer. Idiot, running it
Without oil, excited for the task
Of moving stones. I wanted to be a farmer—
So little of it has to do with soil.
My dog, impatient with my bucolics,
Pants at the door, shrill in her plea
To get to work. Work! She wants to chase
A stick, knowing neither come by
Nor away, nor what to do behind a cow.
My fault, of course, I had the sheep, but
Was too busy making books, throwing pots,
Mending fences just until the coming of the rain,
Busy fanning the 'Round Up' back into my neighbor's
Beans, and keeping the miners at bay; so
She bays and hunkers down behind her stick.
No doubt now I'll get papers served
For using a proprietary proper noun. By the way,
Prosperity fills the space around us. All you need
To do is see it, use it, and feel the wealth. My fifty
Dollars get me sixty years of know how. The old father
Points to the picture on my cell phone, "Remove this
And this; tie this back and unplug these wires.
There are four bolts underneath, catch the fluid
That will come out of this hose. Oh, we'll get it back
Together, Friend; that's obvious. Farming is fixing."
I lean back on the grass unready to wrench.
The sunlight washes out the how-to
On my computer screen. The manure builds up
In the barn; if I can get it to the spreader
And into the field, I might just prosper yet again.

The Bloody Bib of the Red-Breasted

Grosbeak bespeaks at least some
    Past treachery. Not Ugolino, not Stalin,
But one wonders what sort of being
    Spends a life as the astral body of a stained bird
Combing the tips of the new-sprung, soulful
    Plants we live on. This one's looking
At himself in my plate glass, not a little
    Affronted, puffed-up, as I rise a dense
Shadow behind the mirror of his world.
    He retreats a few wing beats to the wire fence
And returns. I move again, a great menace
    Backing up his doppelgänger, and he's down
Valley in no time seeking out the steeple
    Of St. Mark's Lutheran Church. He doesn't
Like what he sees, that shadow welling up
    Before him and so within him, like so many
Church-goers who fertilize their chemical lawns
    Each spring, and me with my nettle tea.

Shepherd's Lament

Can't say what the oldest will get—there's a list,
    He's been told, but it's gone when he gets there.
In many ways that's the best story, surprisingly!
    You see he's like a bromeliad that needs a constant

Change of a fast-draining soil and dim light.
    Santa was like that and look at all the good he did.
Some call Santa a bastard, and say he came late to the war
    And found himself staring at two enemies—imperialists!

He had trouble with his gun holster and the cut of his uniform.
    His medals tasted of mint. He started the campaign forlorn.
His patent leather boots were soggy. His socks a little dense

With fungus—I say all the stoic love in the world couldn't
    Change that. I once had my best crook come unraveled
In the rain. I know what it cost, but I shouldn't care.

Fin de Siècle

Everyone's heliotropic, even on this gray day—
    same as it ever was. I'm still doing it the old way.
I'm happy about Christmas, which is new for me:
    fake tree with a crooked trunk, a few handmade cards
For ornaments. My son is delighted by new pajamas.
    Then, of course, there are the elves and gnomes
Who escaped the box just as I opened it. There was nothing
    I could do. They fight nightly when we're not
In the room and hide when we come in. It remains
    the damnedest thing: all night the sounds
Of the most vicious violence without weaponry one
    can imagine (unless candy canes sucked to a point
Count as weapons, and I suppose they do); then as soon
    as I come out of my room, they're taking pains
To hide themselves *and* each other! I was surprised one night
    to see both an elf and a gnome peeking around
The same corner of the couch at me, their little dagger canes
    hidden by their thighs. Why the elf didn't impale the gnome
Right there and be done with it I'll never figure.
    I would guess, since elves fight in the style of angels
And gnomes like those tenacious dwarves (my neighbor
    has *them*), it's a pretty compelling match-up.
Who knows how long it will last. I think we should
    start a fund to keep the old customs alive, don't you?
I'll bet a dime. Who do you think will see me in time?

Due to the Advances of Modern Politics

We know that when we forgive a tree for falling alone
    It does so quietly, so as not to disturb the concert
Of coyotes applauded in a distant quarry by a one-armed
    Stonecutter who wipes his brow with his one cuff
And holds his chisel in his teeth. His image is out
    Of focus in a mirror. Nearby, fleas varnish the withers
Of his cart horse, or donkey. He curries the rump
    With a chestnut husk. The aggregation of stone chips
Carves the hooves to a natural angle. Here's a list
    Of people who must have an inner life: cooks, teachers,
Cashiers and night stockers, drivers, painters and glaziers.
    The ravine into town is full of beige flowers the bees cannot see.
They swerve through the limestone pinnacles flush
    With garments of dust. The Proletariat is marching again
With all six legs this time, along the sills and shutters
    Of our society, the red ones and the black ones, working
Their mandibles in the roadways, in the government buildings,
    Through the parks and into the open band shells. Easy targets
To each other, and easier still—in AM or FM— to the pundits
    Guiding us home across the bridges and freeways. All quite easy.

John Torgrimson

Vietnam Revisited: A Personal Journey

On the Mall, a volunteer tells me the panel number and I repeat it in my head as I begin the slow descent toward a great gash in the earth. I can see people gathered in bunches looking up at the black granite. Some are hugging each other. Others quietly crying. A couple of veterans are standing vigil. I can see Washington DC all around me, reflected off the shiny blackness. Cumulus clouds dance in the blue sky. My heart is racing.

I feel a strong sense of awe, a somber spiritual feeling like I am at a wake, bearing witness to a terrible tragedy that befell a friend. Most from my generation know someone whose name is carved into the Vietnam Veteran's Memorial: a cousin, brother, father, or hometown son. Some are looking for an explanation, others searching for meaning, and yet, many are there to say goodbye.

I look for Charlie's name on panel W 7 and can't find it. I search and search again, all the names a giant word puzzle. I suddenly feel a sense of suspended belief. Maybe I only imagined he was killed over there, that I helped carry his coffin at the funeral, and I wouldn't find his name here after all. Maybe, somehow it was all a terrible mistake, a bad nightmare.

And then, there it was. It jumped off the stone and all the other 58,000 names suddenly disappeared. Charles H. Meakins was all by itself. I started to cry.

Charles H. Meakins

1. Good vs. Evil

The hot August sun streamed through the tall pines, the gravestones standing quiet vigil as Charlie's family and friends milled around the gravesite. I remember the weight of the casket as we set it on the bier and stepped aside for the priest to say the final prayers.

Charlie was dead. Accidentally killed by the Army's own ordinance on a hillside in Vietnam. Far away from his home and the people who loved him. I looked at his mother and siblings and could see the terrible loss they felt. The folding of the flag that draped the coffin seemed like a sad ending to a life, a sacrifice unfairly offered. The sharp crack of the honor guards' rifles cut into the afternoon's sadness.

I often think how strange the architecture of history is: how the people of a small Asian nation fighting to be free of its colonial past turns into a civil conflict that becomes a proxy war over Democracy versus Communism, good versus evil. The Cold War didn't always make sense, but the specter of a Totalitarian world was motivation enough to bear any cost to stop it. And if we didn't stop it now, where would it all end? Better to fight the Red Menace in the rice paddies in some backwater than on the Main Streets of America, or so the thinking went at the time. "We'll be home by Christmas," was the mantra as Marines waded ashore in DaNang, South Vietnam in March 1965.

So, events years ago—France's colonization of Indochina in the 1800s and the US's support for the French reclaiming Indochina as a colony after World War II—would one day end up on Charlie Meakins' doorstep and end his life in the summer of 1970. In the end, the war did come to Main Street, or at least to Charlie's house in the northwest section of Austin, Minnesota. And to mine as well, 10 blocks away.

We never thought it would find us, but it snuck up on us little by little. In church the priests would ask for prayers to protect our servicemen fighting for freedom in Asia.

The incantations from the celebrants—God Pray for Us, Lord Hear Our Prayer—were intended as a spiritual balm that seemed to negate our complicity in the conflict, implying that we were over there to protect the Vietnamese people from an uncertain future and a life without God's benevolent presence.

Charlie and I were in kindergarten in 1954 when Vietnam was partitioned into north and south following the French defeat at Dien Bien Phu. As teenagers, we saw Vietnam come into our living rooms with the nightly news, about the time our families sat down to supper. We graduated from high school in 1968, the year the Tet offensive swept Vietnam and changed the war, Martin Luther King Jr. and Bobby Kennedy were assassinated, and the antiwar movement was gaining a foothold across the country. The nation would watch in horror that fall as Chicago Mayor Daley's police force bludgeoned unarmed protesters in Grant Park during the Democratic National Convention. In November, Richard Nixon was elected President.

America was in chaos. The leaders who inspired the youth of this country were dead. There was very little trust in the establishment to solve the problems of civil rights, poverty, and social justice. Organizations like the Black Panthers and Students for a Democratic Society rose up in response to the establishment's policies. Meanwhile, American exceptionalism was on trial in the rice paddies in Vietnam.

2. Main Street

Charlie and I were high school friends. Both of us lost our fathers at an early age, a silent secret we shared as we navigated through adolescence. Where I was unsure and sometimes anxious, Charlie was confident and a risk taker; while I was athletic, Charlie was a fixer and tinkerer. He was known as Charlie Tuna, named after the popular cartoon spokesman for *Starkist Tuna*. And in many ways, he resembled the cocksure character's swagger, although he lacked the boisterous conman's over-the-top style. Neither one of us had much interest in our studies. After you lose your father, getting a D is not the crisis it once was: "What the fuck, we passed didn't we"?

He had a regular adult job as a chef at the Austin Hotel while going through high school. He grew up working at his family's roadhouse, The Village, outside of town along Highway 16, pumping gas and learning the restaurant trade along with his ABC's. As a senior in high school Charlie owned a car, a snowmobile and a motorcycle. He ran them hard, and he ran them fast. It was not unusual for Charlie to pop over to my house out of the blue and say, "Hey, let's go for a spin." I lived a few blocks from the freeway and five minutes later we were going one hundred miles an hour down I-90 on his Suzuki S6. Another time in the middle of a snowfall he buzzed over on his snowmobile at nine at night. "It's time to explore the whiteness," he said as explanation. "Dress warm."

We didn't hang out on a daily basis as many friends did, but every few weeks we would spontaneously do something together. After school one day in our junior year, he invited me over to his house where he surprised me with the just released Sergeant Pepper's Lonely Hearts Club Band. We sat on his bed in his upstairs bedroom, smoked cigarettes, and listened to the album from start to finish.

After high school, I stayed in Austin to attend community college, while Charlie headed west, enrolling at Orange Coast State College in Costa Mesa, California. We both got low numbers in the Selective Service lottery draft, and it wasn't long before our II-S student deferments became I-A classifications. According to the government, we were now available for military service.

While I was getting ready to fight the draft, I heard from Charlie's sister, Colleen that he was considering enlisting. She asked me to come over and meet with her and her mom, Doris. We stood in the kitchen and discussed Charlie's options. I told them I didn't believe in the war and planned on filing to become a Conscientious Objector. One no longer needed to file for a CO on religious grounds but could oppose the war on moral grounds as well. Communist or not, I was opposed to our involvement in Vietnam, war in general, and the military industrial complex in principle. It turned out that I was one of more than 500,000 young men who applied to be a Conscientious Objector during the Vietnam conflict. After my visit with Doris and Colleen, I called Charlie in California and we talked surf and sunshine, beaches and girls. He was living with a high school friend of ours eking out a living and getting by. Eventually we got around to discussing the draft. He didn't see any good choices other than enlisting and getting it over with. He didn't like college and didn't see any other way forward.

3. Service to Country

Charlie enlisted in the Army in fall of 1969 and arrived in Vietnam on March 24, 1970, assigned to C Company, based in Tay Ninh Province, fifty miles northwest of Saigon along the Vietnam— Cambodian border. Tay Ninh is home to the Cao Dai religious sect, an amalgamation of Buddhism, Christianity, Confucianism, Islam, and Judaism. Its Papal See was the Cao Dai Great Temple with its all-knowing divine eye that looks out over the faithful. During the Vietnam War, the Cao Dai had its own army that was loosely aligned with the South Vietnamese government.[5]

After in-country processing, Charlie joined his unit on March 29. Amazingly, only three days later, he was awarded the Bronze Star for his valor during an early morning attack on Forward Support Base Illingsworth. The base, located five miles from the Cambodian border near a major infiltration route for the North Vietnamese Army (NVA), was assaulted by a battalion of 400 NVA regulars in the early morning hours of April 1. The battle, described as "hell on earth," cost the NVA two hundred dead; twenty-five known US losses and fifty-four wounded in action. Eight soldiers in Charlie's unit were among the killed in action. One soldier received the Medal of Honor for his heroic actions that day.[6] Charlie's unit spent the next few months moving from one forward support base to another, all of them in the Tay Nihn—Cambodia border area.

In May of 1970, President Richard Nixon authorized US troops, accompanied by Army of the Republic of Vietnam (ARVN) soldiers, to intercept NVA supplies along the Ho Chi Minh Trail in neighboring Cambodia.

The news created a firestorm of protests on college campuses throughout the United States. One protest at Kent State ended with the killing of four students by Ohio National Guardsmen adding fuel to an already growing chorus of opposition to the Vietnam war. Even Congress got into the act, passing legislation limiting the president's war-making powers.[7] Nixon defended his actions by saying that the intervention would give the US more time to train ARVN troops in anticipation of a gradual withdrawal of American soldiers from Vietnam.

On May 22, 1970, Charlie's unit crossed into Cambodia and remained based there until the end of June, searching for enemy caches of arms and supplies. The Army awarded Charlie its Commendation Medal for Valor for his efforts on the 12th to 14th of June while on patrol clearing enemy weapons.[8]

4. Moral, Ethical or Religious Grounds

The Selective Service office was located in a third-floor walkup on south Main Street in Austin. The room was cavernous with very few furnishings, just file cabinets, a secretary's desk, and a large table where the Draft Board conducted its business.

When I told the secretary I wanted to apply for Conscientious Objector status, she replied, "Are you sure you want to do this? I don't think anyone has ever done this before." Not wanting to explain anything to her, I took the paperwork and went home.

So, tell me, did a Vietnamese peasant care if his government was communist or not, if it could give him the opportunity and hope that he and his family's lives would improve? Was it really better to be dead than Red as the saying went? These were the thoughts that ran through

---

[5] A major scene in Graham Greene's novel *The Quiet American* takes place at the Cao Dai temple.

[6] Virtual Wall www.virtualwall.org; The book *Fire Base Illingsworth: An Epic True Story of Remarkable Courage Against Staggering Odds* by Philip Keith documents the battle.

[7] On June 24, 1970 Congress repealed the Gulf of Tonkin resolution. By June 30 all US troops were pulled out of Cambodia.

[8] Virtual Wall www.virtualwall.org

my head as I prepared my case for why the war was wrong and why I couldn't serve.

My mother was quietly supportive of my efforts. She knew the harsh realities and sheer randomness of war, having lost a brother in the Battle of the Bulge in World War II. At 19, I was just becoming a man— one finding himself taking a stand opposed to his own country's policies.

"You could enlist in the Navy," my mom said one day, fearing the ramifications of my decision. Small town Midwest attitudes about Vietnam were supportive of our collective duty to serve. Who were we to question whether the war was right or wrong? Didn't we owe it to previous generations who gave so much to preserve our freedoms? The Draft Board, consisting of three World War II veterans, grilled me on why I was applying for a CO

"Would I defend my family if it were attacked?"

"Yes, of course," I said. "But Vietnam has nothing to do with my family."

"Was India justified in going to the defense of East Pakistan (Bangladesh) in its war of independence from Pakistan?"

"I don't know anything about East Pakistan," I told them. "I do know that America's involvement in Vietnam is wrong and that thousands of innocent civilians are dying."

The questions continued in a similar vein about World War II, the Nazis and the Japanese, and the Commies someday invading America.

When asked by the three-man Draft Board if I would be willing to perform alternative service, I said I would. In the end, they turned down my request for Conscientious Objector status concluding that I was only trying to avoid the draft.

Soon after the decision was handed down, I received my notice to go for my pre-induction physical. Security was tight at the Federal Building in Minneapolis following a recent bombing of the building by a radical fringe element, as I and a large number of young men followed yellow footprints painted on the floor

from one medical station to another. Dressed in nothing but our underwear and shoes, and carrying a sheaf of papers, we spent the next four hours being certified "ready and fit" to serve in the United States Army.

I was not surprised by the Draft Board's decision. I returned to college and resumed my studies planning to appeal the decision. I was taking a full load of classes and working five hours a day in a factory making stereo speakers. I had ninety days to file, and by law I was entitled to two appeals.

Then the unexpected happened. Perhaps it was a coincidence, but after Nixon's forays into Cambodia, the Selective Service System went into a mysterious period of review. A few months later I received a letter from the government stating that my status had been reclassified I-H—*registrant is not currently subject to processing for induction or alternate service.* [9]

To this day I don't know the reason I received the new classification. Did the government create it out of the blue? Did they want to get so-called troublemakers out of the system? Protests were at fever pitch and the government was coming under fire for the disproportionate number of draftees coming from poor lower-class families like mine, at a time when the war was not going well. Nonetheless, while the draft continued, my struggle with the US government seemed to be over.

5. The Arc of History

Charlie's unit continued to patrol near the Cambodian border over the summer. Charlie was about six months into his one-year tour of duty, a veteran soldier, when tragedy struck.

At night when units were out on patrol, they would set up perimeter defenses that included setting Claymore mines around their base of operations. On August 25, 1970, a South Vietnamese Army Kit Carson Scout accidentally detonated a mine. Charlie and another soldier standing nearby were killed instantly. [10]

The headline in the Austin Daily Herald read: **Austin man killed in S. Vietnam.** At that time,

---

[9] In an official government publication about the draft dated 1971, I-H is not listed as a Classification Designation.

[10] Virtual Wall www.virtualwall.org

Charlie was the eighteenth casualty of the war from Mower County. A week later I was a pallbearer at his funeral.

I drove by Charlie's house recently, a tall two-story facing north on a corner lot, now painted a garish royal blue instead of the white it used to be. I parked the car and thought about those troubling times.

How could two kids cut from similar cloth end up on such different journeys? Was it easier to say, "Yes, I will go," than, "No, I won't."? We both did what we felt we had to do, but the outcomes were very different.

Some of my friends who opposed the war ended up serving in Vietnam despite their misgivings. I remember a drunken night out when a friend and I tried to talk our buddy into skipping out. He had just got his induction notice and had two weeks to report. "We'll go to Canada with you. This whole thing is bullshit. No one thinks this war is valid. What did the Vietnamese ever do to us? You give us the word and we're by-ya."

My friend was a star athlete, president of his senior class, stuck between the ramifications of serving or not serving. What would people think of him if he left? How could he tell his dad, who served in New Guinea during the Pacific campaign in World War II, that he wasn't going to serve? What did he feel that he owed this town? This country? Why was it so hard to say, "No, I won't go?" He went.

I wasn't a protester or marcher. I didn't join any sit-ins or break into the Draft Board to destroy records. I didn't plant bombs in government buildings. I was too busy trying to survive. While I had doubts about the existence of God and my Catholic faith, my religious upbringing played a role in my filing for a CO Embedded in my mind was the notion that war was man's ultimate failure to resolve conflict and, in the case of Vietnam, allowing people the right of self-determination.

Disagreeing is a choice. Once I decided to become a Conscientious Objector, I made the decision that it was a journey I would have to make to the very end, regardless of whatever the result would be. Even if it meant going to prison.

Looking back at the 19-year-old I was at the funeral, I remember how difficult it was to put the death of a friend in some kind of context, especially one taken in a war that I was opposed to. I resented the military attendant at the funeral and his platitudes that Charlie's death was not in vain. But I fought my anger and tried to picture Charlie both as a good friend and a soldier. He was tall with an engaging smile and a hell of a lot of fun to be around. And, yet he could be tough when he needed to be. I don't doubt that he was a brother to his comrades-in-arms and had their backs as they had his. Most of them were put in a place they probably didn't want to be in, left to make the most of a bad situation, fighting to stay alive to see another day. He was twenty years old, with his whole life in front of him.

Vietnam found my generation, its arc of history conceived years before. The Gulf of Tonkin incident was written into the stars long before the false reports emerged of North Vietnamese boats firing on the USS Destroyer Maddox, which precipitated America's bombing of Vinh in central Vietnam. America was looking for a place to make a stand against international communism and found it 6,000 miles away.

We would one day learn with the release of the Pentagon Papers by Daniel Ellsberg how successive presidents deceived the American public about Vietnam. Each of them would put America's sons and daughters in harm's way in a war that they knew was unwinnable. More than 58,000 of them would die and thousands more would be physically and psychologically disabled. It is estimated that more than 3 million Vietnamese died during what the Vietnamese refer to as "America's War."

In 1986, sixteen years after Charlie's death, I was in Washington DC attending a conference on refugee resettlement.[11] I was working at the time with a charity resettling Indochinese refugees Minnesota. My primary caseload was made up of Vietnamese Boat People.

---

[11] It is estimated that more than one million Vietnamese fled Vietnam between 1975 and 1995. They were referred to as "Vietnamese Boat People" because many fled the country by sea.

It was a short trip from Georgetown University, host of the conference, to the Vietnam Memorial. I remember looking futilely up at the Wall for Charlie's name. Perhaps that is the beauty of Maya Lin's controversial design, the seemingly random nature of the names bunched together just as they fell in combat.

Charles H Meakins' name is on the Wall next to 58,000 other Americans - Panel W 7, Line 6.

Editor's Note: John went on to serve his country as a Peace Corps Volunteer. He later worked with refugees in Southeast Asia and in the US

How to watch a meteor shower

They come like wings—no—like light around   *Eyes, mind open, waiting.*
  birdwings in flight, chanceled stars, flowering
  sapphire incarnations, and we alone in
  night's embrace all blessed with fireflies
  suturing the darkness whole, breathless in
  the grace of grasses, eyes widening to
  admit the universe, the moon a silent   *The Zodiac cannot guide*
you.
  O of wonder.   *A meteor comes all in*
now.

They come like strings
  strumming the night's guitar, shivering the
  tambourine moon, our "Ah!" in-
  breath, inscape, purer than prayer   *Try not to guess. This is*
like
  or rush of bells through crystal air,   *worrying one line of a*
poem
  down paths of ecstatic fire and sand,   *till you ruin the whole.*
  return time to eternity in grateful quest,
  the moon a silver coin worth all spending.

They come, pulsing blood and agony   *Here the sky's ocean*
  unfathoms
  shed for us, gold and silver snakes,   *the night.*
  holy outriders of the Fall
  that briefly bare the sky-blue gentian,
  while high, high above all longing,
  the moon a gentle compass rose of love.

Let them plunder the night from darkness,   *Do not worry about time.*
  There
  and carve an answer to the silence.   *Is nothing to transcend.*
  Thou gatherest here your sighs to angels,
  the moon a sudden chrysalis
  weaving the skeins of time.

The "water witch"

Her divining rod Ariels the wind,
    seeking the holy center deep below.
    One flick of the stick's bright tongue
    and her quest will be complete.
The owner and the neighbors follow
    at a slight, distrustful distance.
    One spindly old woman points to her head
    and mouths one word: "Touched!"
Dark below, the water stirs with longing,
    for it is incomplete without a thirst.
    The stick mesmers the wind to stillness,
    and then it—lowers to the greening earth.
A sudden light ignites the air.
    Her palms bleed, she faints in the waiting grass.
    The neighbors gasp, the Baptist minister
    prays that he need not touch her.
The divining rod claws the ground.
    The tree roots quiver, sense an end to drought.
    The owner jerks a thumb back,
    and the steam shovel curses into life.

Of a man skating

Once you were master of distance near,
    equilibrium that balanced you whole,
    the sound of your skates gliding on diamonds,
    to spin then—stop—and feel the world
    whirl round a prelude to your song,
    the holy decibels of your steel
    carving signatures of dream--
    then silence, then the echoing woods.
You return now, all these years later,
    hoping to find those echoes again,
    but the time aches, the skates sting deep,
    and you're thinking—How retrace those
    perfect, thoughtless patterns you wrote here
    once, so long ago even the snow
    cannot remember? Perhaps an echo
    never finds a home.
It is gone now, that forever circle you
    made, or may have only dreamed,

that encircled all the others. Still, you
    attempt the leap—concentrate!—Perhaps
    time will collapse and fold up like
    a pocket telescope. No. Divinity
    never will be willed, and you must learn
    to live in time and memory.
Here, where a teenage girl tries and tries,
    awkward, chubby, flailing arms—she falls
    and falls, picks herself up, curses, tries again,
    tears avoiding her acne, the whole sky
    an isolate darkness, and yet you imagine
    her matured into grace, head far back,
    arms in perfect equilibrium, someday,
    spinning her heart to joy.

The antique children

The antique children
    are lined like convenient deaths
    on a Victorian love seat
    in my grandmother's store in the country.
Their eyes are jewels that glitter sinister moons,
    apricot cheeks, but foreheads cracked with time,
    their smiles drowned long ago, lips parted, mouthing
    a silence—plump, prettied and alone.
I believe they are gifted, clued to the dark,
    hands clutching an emptiness like gold.
    Have they ever touched daylight?
    Is there some memory they cannot say?
Late at night I hear them
    walking from aisle to aisle,
    awkward, desperate as asylum echoes,
    searching for any door.
I cover my ears and try not to scream
    as their intricate fingers claw at my lock,
    while their rocking horse, strung from the ceiling,
    rides away, rides away, rides away…

 he Canadian government's reaction to the pandemic has been for the most part ineffective. The wide-ranging restrictions have had many adverse effects. It comes as no surprise that the results of our government mandates have seen an increase in domestic violence. The opioid epidemic is the worst it's ever been. Depression, financial strain are also resultant effects. The economy has had vast setbacks. Local merchants were ordered to shut down their businesses numerous times. Students/Children during the pandemic were not allowed to play sports, play an instrument or sing, and they were least less likely to become sick and die from the virus. Some citizens were subjected to watch their loved ones die via skype! The psychological implications of our government control have yet to be seen. The list goes on and on.

One could argue all these points and disprove them, but one becomes cynical and begs to ask a question: Who would be the ones commissioning the reports to negate them?

If our leaders would have taken greater care of our seniors, those with comorbidities and those at high risks with little or no immunity defenses from the onset, it would have made life much easier for the majority of our citizens who were subjected to unnecessary and ineffective mandates.

On the other hand, the types of pushbacks we had during the pandemic were absurd and ineffective. Namely the protests based on conspiracies; they hardly provided a solution. The freedom convoy trekking to Ottawa did not share the same sentiment as the majority of the Canadian people, to drop all mandates; it was ill-founded from the get-go. The truckers who hunkered down in Ottawa for weeks were *Waiting for Godot*. But Trudeau our Godot, never did make an appearance to address the convoy and that resulted in having rig owners take the law in their own hands as they proceeded to blockade goods and services to the US Trudeau did nothing for days until it became apparent that the truckers were going to crouch and make their home at the border indefinitely. Needless to say, this was not a sensible rally.

So, what to do for the next time a virus lands on our continent? It's been said that we should learn to live with any deadly virus that makes its debut. But that kind of narrative sounds dangerous as it implies that we sit and wait until the next round comes along and then deal with it, hardly a way to be proactive. It seems like we should be preparing now and build infrastructures and train personnel to better service and protect the most vulnerable and in turn let the children play and run the economy without stoppage.

But will this be top priority with the present war in the Ukraine? Will the country's healthcare be put on hold once again?

April Storm

While the oatmeal simmers
I listen to the weather report from Calgary:
sub-zero in Peace River, ground blizzards near Red Deer,
black ice on Crowsnest Pass.

Here on the Flathead
the snow is more cloud than frost
misting on the thawed grass.
Juncos search for grit in the woodshed
scratching through pinechips.
Chickadees flit around the empty feeder
demanding breakfast.

Out on the road
neighbors drive to work.
Slush slurs the clatter of Sam's diesel.
Swirling snow blurs the strobe
of the school bus.

I should get busy too.
There's brush to burn and
machines that need wrenching.
A shopful of shelved projects.
A bill from the bank
on the kitchen table.

But today I'll consider the wisdom
of the cottonwoods by the well
who are waiting for a better day
to open their tarred buds.

Let the world go about its business.
I'll take what the storm offers:
A morning to enjoy a cedar fire
while the snow slips off the roof.
A moment to rest
before beginning the task of summer.

Work Truck

When it was time to sell the Dodge
I considered washing it
but a cold front was blowing in
and I didn't want to risk freezing the hydrant.

I thought about straightening
the right rear corner of the bed,
bent when I backed into a dozer track
or a log deck, I forget which,
but decided that tackling the job
with my customary body repair tools—
a hi-lift jack, a comealong
and an assortment
of sledgehammers, prybars and wood blocks—
would just make it worse.

So I jammed the taillight into its mangled socket,
cinched it down with a couple self-tapping screws,
and wiped off the winter's roadfilm
with a musty sweatshirt I discovered behind the seat.

It's a work truck for Chrissakes, I muttered,
as I parked it by the mailbox and
duct-taped a chartreuse,
hand scrawled, For Sale sign
in the driver's window.
Why try to doctor it up?

Walking back to the shop, I hoped
If I ever fell prey to an undertaker
He'd do the same for me:
Dress me in my woods clothes,
with my hands in the open,
exposing every stitch, scar and raw hangnail.
And don't bother straightening
the warped, aching finger
I always threatened to amputate,
but never did.

The Marten on the Gutpile

The ravens war
and scatter into the timber,
but the marten stands his ground,
perched on the cow's stomach.

Whiskers glossed with tallow.
Orange throat
smudged with blood.

He retreats to a spruce limb
when we start skinning,
snarls at the camprobbers
who appear
in the absence of ravens.

They eat flakes of ribfat
while we bone the carcass
on the peeled hide.

I toss a slice of liver
to the marten.
He caches it under
a lodgepole windfall
and climbs back to his post
growling deep
in his scrawny chest.

When we're finished
he watches us
squirm into our packs
and line out for the trail.

Before we're out of sight
he's nosing through the intestines
haloed by jays.

Wise River
November 2007

Additional dialogue by Jules Genelle Celeste, Vivienne Chaconas, Amethyst Cucumber Rose, Raven Bloodknight, & Flint Vasquez

haracters

Abraham: A man.
Philomon: Another man.
Trash Can Man: A man who lives in a trash can.

Abraham and Philomon are in a pub, waiting for Samuel Beckett to arrive at the small bookshop across the way, that they can see through the window.

Abraham: So what do you think about the reading?

Philomon: We've come. We'll wreck it. *Takes a drink, then holds the beer bottle up in the air.*

Abraham: We are waiting for Samuel Beckett. *Raises his own beer glass.*

Philomon: Where are all the dead people from?

Abraham: Where? Which?

Philomon: In the pub. I saw them. Maybe they were in our glasses. We drank them. *Looks into his empty glass, holding it up like a telescope.*

Abraham: Aye! That's why they call 'em spirits. *Drinks from a bottle of beer.*

Philomon: Drank me a ghost today.

Abraham: Depends on the proof.

Philomon: I thought the proof was in the pudding. Never seen no ghosts there though.

Abraham: You're not looking hard enough.

Philomon: Looking hard enough at what?

Abraham: The pudding. Are you looking out your eye?

Philomon: Let's look out there.

Abraham: and Philomon go to the alleyway near the pub. A Trash Can Man is poking his head out of a small aluminum trash can.

Trash Can Man: I know Samuel Beckett. *Drunkenly.* When I saw him, he walked down Bourbon Street dressed like the Queen.

Philomon: How does he take his tea?

Abraham: *Her* tea?

Philomon: It's tea.

Abraham: Their tea.

Philomon: How many teacups and what was in them?

Abraham: Bourbon on Bourbon Street.

Philomon: The universe, galaxies, I hear they're delicious. Let's hear what the old man has to say.

Abraham: What old man?

Philomon: The man in the trash can.

Trash Can Man: Me.

Philomon: Yeah, whatever you are

Abraham: We want to know what you think.

Trash Can Man: Galileo was an ass.

Abraham: Your mother.

Trash Can Man: My mother what?

Abraham: Your mother gave birth to you and created something from nothing.

Trash Can Man: Do you have something you want me to tell Mr. Beckett?

Abraham: Tell him you never saw us. And if you see my father, tell him the same.

Philomon: How big is that trash can?

Trash Can Man: Big enough to fit on the head of a pin. *Closes trash can lid, exiting conversation.*

Abraham: Something's not right. *Takes off hat. Another hat is underneath it. Takes off necklaces, shakes them out, adds to pile. Takes off jacket, turns it inside-out, looks through sleeves, checks pockets. Takes off vest, reverses it, puts it back on. Takes it off again. Unbuttons button-up shirt, looks through pockets, takes off t-shirt, undoes straps of brassiere, puts hands in air, questioningly. Starts to unzip fly.*

Philomon: Stop!

Abraham: You're in no position to tell me when to stop or to go. Or to Gogo.

A line of Gogo dancers dance across the stage, passing by Abraham: like he doesn't exist.

Abraham: I think I will stop-stop then. It could be perpetual where you don't ever … *Pause. Nods twice …* Or stop-stop either.

Philomon: Not until we're dead.

Abraham: I can't wait that long.

Philomon: Speaking of which, where is the *author*?

Abraham: *Points to sky.* There's the author.

Philomon: Still on the plane.

Abraham: In the error of existence.

Philomon: Maybe if we're good, he'll come.

Abraham: Then we're off to a miserable start. *Keeps undressing, taking off jeans, animal print leggings, naughty stockings with garters.*

Philomon: You know it's almost Easter, right?

Abraham: Naw, I passed right over it.

Philomon: I'm gonna buy a chocolate cross, and bite right into it.

Abraham: Well I don't need to know about your personal life.

Philomon: He died on the cross.

Abraham: Who did?

Philomon: The guy that gave us bunnies and chicks and chocolate and…*Pauses…*books.

Abraham: *Now down to his underwear – a thong that looks like an elephant, with googly eyes.* What kind of books?

Philomon: All the books. Even the Good Book.

Abraham: Oh, you're a critic now?

Philomon: Peter Rabbit died for your sins.

Abraham: Well, that was rather indecent of me.

Philomon: Sometimes you come, and sometimes you Gogo.

The Gogo dancers appear again, dancing across the stage. This time, they see the old man's trash can, pick it up, and Gogo off the stage with it.

Abraham: Come back for me!

Philomon: What now?

Abraham: I forgot you were there.

Philomon: Why?

Abraham: You're very quiet.

Philomon: I'm dancing silently.

Abraham: No, I'm just hard-of-hearing.

Philomon: Oh

Abraham: What?

Philomon: What?

Abraham: Well that's very rude.

Philomon: *Walks over, examines Abraham:'s pile of clothing. Starts trying things on.*

Abraham: You'll see, any minute!

Philomon: *Sighs in relief.* That's better.

Abraham: What's better for you is worse for me. Then better for me is worse for you. It all comes out in the wash.

Philomon: You mean the stains.

Abraham: I already told you, I don't want to hear about your personal life.

Philomon: Why?

Abraham: I liked you when you were quieter.

Philomon: I liked me when I was quieter too.

Abraham: Well what's better for you is better for me, then.

Philomon: *Tries on watch. Taps it. Holds to ear. Makes stink-face. Throws it back into pile.*

Abraham: That was a very special piece.

Philomon: They all are.

Abraham: You're just jealous 'cuz you haven't got one of your own.

Philomon: One what

Abraham: Never mind. Have it.

Philomon: Nope. Sound's busted. *The sun is rising.*

Abraham: And that's never busted.

Philomon: So far as we know.

Abraham: Does your head ever explode, with all the questions?

Philomon: Never known it to.

Abraham: Could have fooled me.

Philomon: What day do you suppose it is?

Abraham: Today.

Philomon: It's today until forever.

Abraham: Then I'm always right.

Philomon: *Darkly* Tomorrow never comes.

Abraham: But today does go.

Philomon: *Whispers.* Go.

The Gogo dancers come back. This time, they take Abraham: lifting him above their heads. He seems delighted to go.

Philomon: *Puts watch back on.* Well that was interesting. *Pause.* The sun comes. The dancers go. The author never arrives. And here I am, alone between brick walls, caught in an endless today, and wearing someone else's watch, that does not make a sound. What is it all for?

Abraham: *Yells from off-stage* What is it all three?

Philomon: *Lights cigarette.* Or four. *Chuckles* Now I get it. What is it all for? *Flicks the cigarette.* Does it matter? We're here and then gone, like comets, like birds, like specks of dust in the … *pause* … dustbin. Will the author ever get here? And in the meantime, where do we look for salvation? When we come, where do we come from? When we go, where do we … p*auses, thinks* … go-go? *The Gogo dancers come back. This time, they are irritable, not dancing. Abraham is with them, in a pink, puffy robe. They tag some of the walls with spray paint, messages like "Keep Your Dog On A Leash" and "Spay And Neuter Your Pets." They hand Phil a leash. Abraham is on the other end.*

Philomon: What happened?

Abraham: You don't talk about your personal life, and I don't talk about mine.

Philomon: Fair enough.

Abraham: *Opens robe.* I think something's in this, too.

Philomon: Stop!

Abraham: Oh, I forgot you were there.

Philomon: Where?

Abraham: *Points at bookstore.* In line for the laundromat.

Philomon: All hail the mighty author, who cleanseth our clothes.

Abraham: I'm not scumming for your clothes.

Philomon: You're not the author.

Abraham: Well how do you know?

Philomon: Your signature's not worth anything.

Abraham: Well how do you know?

Philomon: Try to sell it to somebody.

Abraham: *Sits down on concrete* Observe. *Puts hand out into air like he's begging. Randomly, a quarter falls from the sky.*

Philomon: It's raining wealth.

Abraham: Enough for the dry!

Philomon: *Takes hat, holds it out.* An apple falls into it. *Phil takes it out and holds it up.*

Abraham: Bad luck, but that was your first try.

Philomon: *Sets the apple on the sidewalk. Shakes the hat out, tries again. This time, a fish falls into it.*

Abraham: Well that's worse, but you've got the charm, coming up.

Philomon: *Takes fish, sets it down onto newspaper, shakes hat out, tries again. A cruddy old watch, like Abraham's, falls in. He takes it out, looks at it.*

Abraham: Is the laundromat closed Sunday?

Philomon: I don't see why they would be. Laundromat ain't sacred.

Abraham: Well check on the door. Someone might have nailed something up.

Philomon: *Walks over. Checks the bookstore's door. No sign.* Looks clear to me, but no author. Laundromat looks open. Even on Sunday, people gotta clean their holey underwear.

Abraham: Well I'm cold. I'm Jimmy-ing the door.

Philomon: All right. Go on in then.

Abraham Opens the door easily, as though it was never locked. It stays open and does not shut, as Abraham gathers up the clothes.

Philomon: Well, let's go in.

Abraham: I wasn't inviting you.

Philomon: I got an invitation from the author.

Abraham: I never sent you a thing.

Philomon: You are not He, the great S.B.

Abraham: Well that's awfully rude of you. A man can be three men at once.

Philomon: Can he?

Abraham: *Ignoring question.* Give me the clothes.

Philomon: Why? What are you going to do with them?

Abraham: Wash. You don't look like you can afford.

Philomon: I can pay you in apples and fish.

Abraham: That's good enough. I'll take them. *Gathers up clothes, apple, fish, and goes inside.*

Philomon: *Attempts to follow. Door closes and locks. The sign that says Open, goes out. The sound of a badly balanced washing machine can be heard.*

Lights go out.

Folk Opera Special Focus — Seven Authors & Poets from the
Literary Renaissance Taking Place in Northfield, Minnesota

I long for the thunder to wake me
For the lightning to shock
to shake me.
For my thoughts to rule this night
For the weather's heartless bite

Because Love

We cannot
go out and have fun
dine without planning at Reunion
attend theater—at all

make a move without risk assessment
celebrate birthdays *en masse*
luxuriate in hugging our friends

escape these four walls
avoid the feeling of entrapment
sing our joys—when Joy itself has fled

We cannot
find a light at the end of this mine shaft
rise to the surface of these deep woes
hope for a future better than our past

see democracy thriving
hear ourselves, the people, calling to each other
shake the unworthy from the seats of power

We must not
stifle our generosity
stymy our will to act
flag in our determination to be and do better

Even if everything seems lost
Even if we can't imagine the dawn we once believed in
Even if compassion and love have been confined to our solitary hearts

We can, despite winter, still
come to the town square
shout from our doorsteps and windows
resist the howls of the haters

Because love in the face of such hatred is the only way
Because without love, buried so deeply within us, we cannot survive
Because we need each other, my loves, at this dark moment in this dark place.

Requiem for the Common Good: Summer 2021

Very hot. Very still.
The pandemic alone moves.
Person to person.
What worked against it
is failing. We are failing.
Not pulling together.
Not holding the line.
Not putting our neighbor
before us. Not loving
each other enough

to risk what we hold dear

for those that we hold dear.
No longer persuading.
Just exasperating.
Throwing up our hands.
Throwing down the gauntlet.
Storming the capitols.
Settling for "I told you so"
even as Death hoists its sickle
over all our squabbling heads.

Sonnet: Better Angel

The words echo in my head, play over
and over and over. I say them aloud,
imagine the forms gratitude and love
take: I conjure them. And revenge. I'm weak:
I can't resist taking down the enemy,
peeling back the skin of their unkindness
unkindly, rooting out the mystery
of cruelty cruelly. I could write an ode
to vengeance, a crown of sonnets to the rack,
pantoums to nail- and eye-plucking that would
shock Goneril and Regan, villanelles
to celebrate in dungeons their spilled blood:
I would sate my atavistic urges.
But I won't: I'll turn to love and gratitude.

Prairie Grasses

Our neighbors have re-planted
the grasses of old. This spring,
as I pass the dead stalks,
they whisper to me
and I understand better what
the people who have always been here
and the ones who came later meant
when they said the prairies spoke to them.
Now we live in a world, a nation,
built on the silence of the fields.

Rainbow Beacon 2021

The separation between us
notwithstanding—
there is always a gap, a gash,
a break—I peer at you,
wait for your light,
for illumination,
to bridge the gulf between us.

Above us, the stars.
Now your beacon
rainbows a swath
of night's dark waters,
glorifies the flimsy
barrier between us:

we prism,
we rainbow,
we become
the light between us.

Holiday Picnic

On Memorial Day the residents
of our Bronx apartment building
would pile into cars for our annual picnic
up in West Chester at Ardsley Park.
It had what for us was a wondrous stream—
frogs, little fish we'd try to catch with nets,
flowers, and stones for fording the chilly water.
Our parents taught us the silly songs
they sang at day camp during the Second
World War, which seemed so distant
from and romantic to us. We learned
that *our ears hang low, yes, they*
wobble to and fro, we can tie them
in a knot, we can tie them in a bow.
We rowed, rowed, rowed our boat
as far as time, music and our ability
to sustain a round would take us.
We ate roasted chicken and hot dogs,
hamburgers with all the fixings,
potato chips (the really old-fashioned
kind, laden with oil), and watermelon.
At sunset we drove back to the Bronx,
exhausted, a little cranky and sticky,
but also sated fully on the joy of living.

The page

is an old friend,
offering the scent
of rainbows past
and the new moon
rising. It waits
with me, a calming
presence, a dream
of what will happen
next, of the possibilities
I, we, might undertake
when you come out
of your office and I
rise to greet you
and we walk out
to reenter the world.

Unredeemable

You've drunk the hydroxychloroquine Kool-Aid:
No other foreign substance will jump-
start your immune system. Nor will others
be protected: You'll let them fend for themselves
unmasked. You say the Lord watches over you.
He loves His children but apparently doesn't
give a damn about the rest of us. There is no vaccine
for willful ignorance, for lack of charity: Your God
wills we abdicate responsible free will.
So you may die
coughing in your bed or waiting for a spot in an over-
whelmed ICU. Or you may infect and kill a loved one
or just another unmasked innocent Child of God.
I see the truth now: There is just no saving The Saved.

Unexpected Gift

for Tom

We didn't expect you—
a late arrival. After we thought
we knew the us that we were.
You altered our calculus—
Cathy and I changed diapers
while Mom went out to work
and Dad adjusted to the fact
of you.
You two hit it off.
Bigtime. You were and are
the most like him. The rest
of us couldn't give a damn
about football or baseball.
We shared movies with Dad,
but you've shared all his passions—
he even coached your Little League team!—
and his affability, gregariousness,
and charm.
So we need you,
baby brother, our littlest and last,
our very best. You can't check out
before the rest of us leave the room.
Your mirth and wit, always tinged
with love. Your letters—so like Dad's
own weepies—full of gratitude
for Beth and the kids, Dad and Mom,
and sometimes even us sibs. We
need you at this dark time, in this
dark year, to lighten our lives.

Tikkun olam?

How do we repair the world we've damaged?
resurrect what we lost through negligence?
set right the garden we have trampled?

I reach across the table, take your hand
in mine to draw from your intelligence
a hint how to repair the world we've damaged.

You look too upon the world we've savaged—
such wars, pollution, hate, indifference:
How can we right the garden we have trampled?

Nature, despairing, has now the forests ravaged—
hot dry winds ignite whole continents.
How do we repair the world we've damaged?

Since waters too rained down and overflowed,
since shores withstood not tide's incontinence—
floods washed away the garden we have trampled.

I look at you and wonder, How've we managed—
so handily despite our good intents—
to flood beyond repair the world we'd damaged,
to burn to ash this garden we have trampled?

Larry Gavin

Paper Wasp and other Poems

The Current of Woodbine

The current of woodbine.
The wound that becomes a scar.
Strafing winds. A compass point.
I am lost in the center of something.
Perhaps everything. The fresh scent
of nettles and undergrowth. Smell it.
Steal it for your own.
It will protect us. It will heal.
It will make us whole.

Memory

I can see the horizon
hear the singing of the wind
through bare trees.
Vibrations. An eternity
in each moment.
There is no lesson here
I realize, just time
passing like wind,
like the heart longing
for a connection
with all that is. I
inhabit this place
solely for remembering.

Paper Wasp

We've spent the summer
looking at each other.
You have grown
to recognize the turn
of
    my mouth,
up at the corners.
Recognizing the emptiness
of this gesture
like the emptiness of air
or the emptiness in my
eyes some days.

We defy gravity. And we
see each other, each
into the heart of each.
I will leave you to live,
but your days are limited
by freezing wind and snow.
I will sing your
loss, but will you see me,
see me, in the long dream
that is winter?

The Moment of Loss

I lost god the first time I
saw a muskrat V across
the surface of Paul's lake,
perfect as any deity
better than any wish
I could have for eternity.
Give me the slow widening
arch of wake from the humblest
of creatures. An example
of good for the sake
of good, good beyond
knowing, beyond reward.
The kind of good that leads
to sainthood, to illumination,

to redemption
knowing lost and reclaimed.
I will search the far shore
when my time is up; confident
that all paths lead back
to that first moment
the moment that loss became me.

Heather Candels

Small Print and other Poems

Interloper

A clown climbed
into my poem without permission.
He just showed up with his red nose,
flaccid balloons and big shoes that I hoped would trip him
but instead stomped on my grapes,
ravaged the lavender
and trampled the fragrant rosemary—
before he smashed the coffee pot
and raided the refrigerator.

His oxidized hair and grease paint
had all dissolved into a sickly orange that flared
with the flames shooting up in the distance where a circus tent burned.

I wondered about the lions.

Small Print

It was always there
the small print
word after word sentence
after sentence paragraph
after paragraph page
after page
too voluminous to absorb
too small to bother with
until one day
it really mattered and there was no recourse
just alphabet soup
boiling letters into disintegration
e's becoming i's or l's
that were once p's or q's?
The blur indecipherable
The regret indescribable

Troubling Deaf Heaven

My prayers scatter
glitter across the sky,
sparkle and twinkle hope,
twirl with the wind,
then vanish.

I wait kneeling,
wonder where these pleas might settle:
mountaintops, or crevices.

I ache for a hand to appear,
—Sistine Chapel style—
an outstretched finger
to trace a path through the stardust
and guide me toward tranquility.

When through the clouds
a broom drops down
and sweeps my requests into an abyss,
my answer unfolds with my hands.

Gospel Billboards.Org

WHERE ARE YOU GOING
HEAVEN OR HELL?
Dial 855-FOR TRUTH

I pull over, dial for answers.
These operators must know:
The Lord told them so!

Regarding eternal salvation,
   —all I need—
to do is to press #2,
and then press #3, hope that Jesus will save me.

Red lights flash
in my rear-view mirror:

Expired registration?
No Visa application?
Here it comes: the sanctimonious proclamation.

I zip up my flame
retardant vest.

I'm ready.

Destination January 20, 2021

I want off this plane

  we're all

                      strapped in

                                 overhead

bins burst open

  oversized baggage
tumbles down ————breaks open our fears

                attendants repair to their
                     jump
         seats buckle up the cockpit is empty the pilot gone

     aircraft banks   we circle

                              and circle and circle
           we've used up all the fuel

                                      babies wail

toilets overflow

      the man before me reclines
until   my teeth cut my knees

      oblivious to my paralysis

                       he's sleeping
           loose food carts careening
down the aisle

  (they said would light up in the rare case of an emergency landing) but there's only the dark and the sick

                           bags are full

     smoke billows from the engines
    are the controllers on strike?
         no signals to guide us in
     as masks drop down our own masks are on
are we now gone   before we plummet

                        to
                  the ground?

Rob Hardy

Song of the White Boy and Another

Song of the White Boy

*Somebody needs to stop telling these white boys that they can be
anything they put their mind to.* —Ijeoma Oluo

Only in my mind can I be a bird
and feel the weight of the air lifting me up,
or a tree so perfectly balanced

between the sustenance of earth and sun.
I can never be the moon
left on all night outside my window,

or even the new-fallen snow.
The innocence of its whiteness eludes me.
Only in my imagination can I be

brown, a woman, anything but a man
the color of chewing gum
stuck to the bottom of a chair.

So I must learn to love in others
what I can never be. I could be
a better man if I put my mind to it.

Instead of building arsenals
and justifications, I could be myself
among other selves, part

of a whole. Why should I be afraid
to be a drop in an ocean of color? Then
I will be a part of the ocean.

Against Simile

I take my coffee out to the porch
and watch the death throes of mayflies
strung up in the paper birch,
like drop spindles
or tangled kites.
The spider here is implied,
like the verb *to be*
often in ancient Greek,
the invisible thread
joining two nominatives,
subject and predicate.
Like an equal sign,
I tell my students.
Then I think of Tom, who says
I'm so sick of similes.
Tom has a new heart,
which of course makes him metaphorical
and not at all like the mayflies.

For Tom Driscoll

S o many Americans have been acting stupidly lately. And lately, people have accused me of being too critical. My response to that assessment of me is, Thank you. I'm proud of my ability to think clearly and rationally.

My health issues and I have been self-isolating for two years now to steer clear of COVID-19 and all its variants. There simply isn't any room in my cramped pandemic space for feigned niceties. So I've been honest and direct in my blogs and social media posts. I've tried to inspire meaningful conversation by posting about what I think matters. Comments regarding how I think society should be responding to issues and people in need don't always go over well. Confessing that I believe in science, that denying science is dangerous, that I have no tolerance for supporting people who condone racist behavior, and that silence in the presence of racism is complicity has become my modus operandi. And a lot of people don't like it.

Recent political and social events have been evidence to me that a society that condones being a silent bystander as tragedy unfolds invites more tragedy to occur. Stating that I believe it is the responsibility of people who have a voice to speak on behalf of those who don't have a voice just feels like something I should do because I desire to be a decent human being in any way I can. I knew long before the pandemic, the killing of George Floyd, and the emergence of America's deep political divide that a lot of people in my social circles have different ideologies than I have. But I fully embrace this quote from Bob Dylan, the non-conformist "voice of a generation." "To be on the side of people who are struggling for something doesn't necessarily mean you're being political."

I have given my friends and family the benefit of the doubt when I've publicly shared my thoughts about the state of our society. I have hoped they would transcend differences in political viewpoints and agree—at the very least—that denying science and supporting bigotry is unacceptable for those desiring a decent society. The word "decent," along with almost everything meaningful I post, turns out to be unexpectedly vulnerable to interpretation these days. Although it isn't my intent, my posts are often considered inflammatory. Some people in my life think it's "decent" to let wealthy people cling to as much wealth as possible via tax loopholes so they can buy more cars or horses while watching others lose their homes and ability to buy food. I have been told that I am "ignorant," "blind," "a sheep," "misguided," and that I am a "libtard" who is helping destroy all that is great about America—even though I'm politically independent. I've been called a communist because I do not agree that living in a free country means we should be allowed to refuse vaccinations because a politician who wants to get reelected tells us to; or refuse to wear a mask around our vulnerable neighbors and freely spread Covid during the height of a pandemic. I have also been accused by someone who has known me for years of supporting a Satan-worshipping cabal that eats babies. I haven't responded because I am stunned that it's even possible for someone I have associated with to believe something like that.

A shockingly high number of friends and family who proudly display their Christian "morality" on social media don't appreciate my posts promoting the idea of adhering to the Golden Rule—treating other people in the way we want to be treated. Cognitive dissonance now seems to reign supreme among so many evangelicals I know. They've stopped sending God's blessings my way and apparently no longer think I'm worth trying to save. I don't imagine they'll be interested in having a relationship with me in the future once this divisive dust from America's social earthquakes settles. They've been told by their various leaders who control their thoughts that people like me are evil because I don't share their ideologies.

They will probably be unable to see me in a positive light—unless their dear leaders tell them to.

I've tried to be sad about the significant number of friends and family relationships I've lost over the past few years as a result of being "critical." But I'm not. I think it's a good thing that I have fewer verbally abusive people in my life whose ideologies are shaped, in large part, by the fact that their TV clickers are apparently stuck on the disinformation network. I am in complete support of having a variety of political ideologies in a democratic society. But I'm afraid of people who don't bother to investigate the truthfulness of what they are told to swallow yet think that their viewpoint is superior to all others. I know from first-hand experience that people who donate their brain matter to leaders who manipulate them for their own benefit, or use them to spread ridiculous conspiracy theories, are dangerous pawns.

Even though I think many of them behave stupidly, I have compassion for people who have been brainwashed because I was once a member of the evangelical world. When I was a teenager, evangelical Christianity was presented to me as a very special gift containing special knowledge that not everyone is in possession of. During a time when appearances were vital and I felt I had no value because I didn't look like Farrah Fawcett, Christie Brinkley, Brooke Shields, or other "beautiful" women of the 1970s and 1980s, possessing the special gift of eternal life and having special access to the teachings found in evangelical Christianity gave me the self-worth I was craving. It didn't matter how physically unattractive I was because being friends with Jesus gave me value that nobody could take away—except for my fellow evangelicals. I understand how many people on the far-right end up thinking—or not thinking—in the way they do.

Christianity is among the most successful marketing campaigns in the history of the world. Peddlers of "the Truth" are adept at selling the message/The Message that those who can suspend their logical system of disbelief and enter a personal relationship with the invisible-yet-everywhere Jesus Christ will be rewarded with eternal life. Sounds like a good deal … but

wait, there's a catch. If you read the fine print on the contract you signed with evangelical Jesus, you will discover that you need to prove that you have cast out the doubting Thomas who dwells within you by joining the nearest evangelical church and giving a minimum of 10 percent of your income for the rest of your life. Otherwise, that compassionate, life-sacrificing deity you just entered into a relationship with will … will what, push you off the Praise-Jesus-Hallelujah bandwagon you just hopped on? No, Jesus won't do that, but many of the Christian thugs who follow him will shove you off that bandwagon if you don't hand over your money and your mind.

I found the evangelical world I experienced to be filled with mafioso-type personalities, and I'm not at all surprised that, with the way Donald Trump engaged in Mafia-style business practices before becoming President of the United States, he found his enthusiastic base in the evangelical far-right pockets of America. Trump's business model was eerily similar to what I experienced in evangelical Christianity. Every evangelical church I tried to become a member of had its bullies who would strongarm members into doing what they were told. If they didn't comply, they were called names, humiliated, and cast out of the fold. I understand that acceptance motivates many of the evangelical pawns caught up in the far-right movement. And I still know how to speak their language, but I simply don't have the charisma or influence to compel them to start viewing life through a logical lens. My interaction with people on today's far-right end of the political spectrum and my desire to demonstrate another way of treating people is pointless. I don't have anything as seductive as eternal life to offer them for becoming a convert to the logical side of American life. All I have to offer is being able to sleep in on Sunday mornings and having 10 percent more income to spend elsewhere—maybe on a new TV with a clicker that allows access to more than Fox Broadcasting. If I had to choose, I'd rather travel through life completely alone than in lockstep with people who experience power by preventing others from living their best possible existence and tell followers how they must talk, dress, and spend their money.

I encountered some wonderful people on my journey with Jesus who happened to have conservative political perspectives. And I still have friendly connections with lots of conservative people. But I'm so thankful for the multitude of abusive experiences I had in the far-right evangelical world that moved me to where I am today on the political spectrum. One charismatic evangelical told me that I had been afflicted with rheumatoid arthritis because I was a sinner who God despised, and if I would just repent, I would be healed. An evangelical pastor, who held church services in the basement of her home and prophesied about the date of her upcoming death and resurrection, said my acne was a result of my rebellious nature, that I had impurities coursing through my blood and my soul. She said if I would just learn how to conform and become more engaged in the church, my skin would be healed. I was actually accused of being a witch by my peers and a campus pastor at the Baptist college I attended. I was gossiped about, ostracized, and even spit on because I had been raised Catholic and had a knack for "predicting" the future. Had I been raised Baptist and dressed in a more churchy way, I probably would have been called a prophet. I wasn't familiar with the terminology at the time, but today I believe that my keen pattern recognition abilities and sharp critical reasoning skills that my parents instilled in me at a young age have always allowed me to have a pretty good sense of what the future consequences of an action might be. I stood out among my peers for being someone who called attention to situations that were causing harm to people and would result in other bad outcomes. My habit of shining a light on problematic situations irritated my evangelical circle. There were a handful of people of color at my Baptist school. I was friends with all of them and felt helpless when there was nothing I could do to improve their experience on our mostly-white, mostly-racist Christian campus. One of my Black friends had a tendency to call out people for their questionable Christian behavior. One of his punishments for speaking out was having the Christian guys in his dorm defecate in his pillowcase.

Nobody pooped in my pillowcase during college. But I frequently got shoved off the holy-roller bandwagon for doing things that deviated from the evangelical norm. A lot of the students on my campus were drinking, doing drugs, and having sex, but they were skilled at appearing "evangelical" and talking the talk, so they were never rejected for deviating. I never got the hang of walking and talking like an evangelical and was repeatedly made to pay for not blending in. I'm a very forgiving person, so I repeatedly forgave my Christian abusers because I thought that's what my friend Jesus would do. But at a certain point, getting pushed to the ground and trampled by Christians finally knocked some sense into me. It awakened the skeptic in me who screamed that it's not okay to be manipulated and abused "in the name of Jesus." I realized that a lot of people had discovered how to use the evangelical Christianity machine to get their piece of power over others. And, spoiler alert, I also became aware that evangelical Christianity doesn't actually have anything special to offer that people can't find by simply reading the westernized version of the Bible on their own. There's no middleman needed. Evangelical Christianity is simply a masterfully marketed club like Tupperware or Mary Kay cosmetics that allows lots of people to make a comfortable living while experiencing some form of power over others who surrender their money and minds. And America's far-right politicians have mastered mankind's ability to profit from Christianity.

I'm fortunate that I could eventually find my way back to a logical life because my parents instilled the message in me when I was young that I should question everything and consider the consequences before jumping on any bandwagon. They showed me how to have original thoughts and create my own vehicle for change. It's unfortunate that when I was a teenager, I rebelled against my parents' logic and didn't embrace their rational message when I impulsively became a born-again Christian. But the critical thinking skills they taught me when I was young allowed me to eventually find myself again as an adult. Now that I'm steering my own course, I've often found myself heading the opposite direction of the mainstream—and definitely in the opposite direction of evangelicals—with the mission of accomplishing something beneficial for society.

The only hope I see for my country to move forward again with the momentum of a truly great nation is for Americans to quit acting so stupidly. It is imperative that our children be taught to pause before jumping on a popular bandwagon fueled by irrationality and a desire for acceptance. Acquiring critical thinking skills will help them eventually become smart voters as adults—adults who don't thoughtlessly hand our precious democracy over to an autocrat who has no respect for our Constitution and drives an entertaining bandwagon. Those kinds of bandwagons may have a tantalizing amount of power at the beginning of their course, but they tend to run over people instead of respecting others sharing the road through life. The reach of the toxic fumes that those attention-getting bandwagons emit extends well beyond our country's borders. We must quit setting bad examples for citizens of other nations. (Sorry, Canada, for teaching you how to be wacky and inspiring your occupation of irrationality.) The whole world would benefit from every American learning to respond to emerging matters with critical reasoning, striving to honestly address social problems, and committing to elevating humanity at every opportunity so that we can all find our way to a path of personal progress.

Becky Boling

Elvis is in the Building and Other Poems

Elvis Is in the Building or How I Moved My Mother to Minnesota

Mission: Extraction of Mother from roost in Evansville, Indiana. Relocation in Minnesota. Prognosis? Difficult.

Packing.
Closets are scary to fans of horror and to anyone who has to move. You can get lost in them for hours and still not find the back wall. It's like Narnia but without the treacle.

Mother Boxed. Moving van loaded. Papers signed. Apartment evacuated. Life in Limbo. Travel Imminent.

Transfer of Principle Asset Accomplished. "Package Mom" secure on temporary premises. Arrival of household goods and furnishings pending.

Boxes have taken Apartment hostage, threaten to colonize the senior housing facility. Recycling called to the rescue. Dust flies up nasal cavities. Drawers, overtaxed, creak on the verge of exhaustion. Time counts down, and Stuff is winning over Space. Is there no hope? Will it all fit? Can we reach the bathroom? Where did we put the pillows?

Mom fusses at corners, cranes her neck to look inside half-emptied boxes, shuffles behind my husband with her walker and peers round his shoulder.

"Mom, what's wrong?" I ask.

She points at a box sitting on a box perched on another box.

"Are those my cookbooks?"

"We unpacked your cookbooks yesterday, remember? They're in the bookcase." I nod at the tall four-shelf wooden case with beveled glass doors entirely filled with Betty Crocker's, Amish, Better Homes, Pioneer Woman, and others.

"That's not all of them. There have to be more." She frowns, and this serious expression reminds me of my grandma, her mother. The same nose—sharp and long—the same high forehead, the same thin lips. Age has exaggerated those features she shares with her mother, and I wonder what I would think if I looked at myself right now in the bathroom mirror.

"You're kidding me," I say.

Her frown deepens. She used to be taller than me, but now we stand, eye to eye.

"I've looked through them and it's not there." She juts her chin forward and narrows her eyes as if challenging me to contradict her.

"What's missing?"

"Elvis."

Doug and I turn in the same moment and exchange looks.

"My Elvis Presley Cookbook. I can't find it anywhere."

Somewhat relieved, I smile in what I hope is a reassuring way. "We've got a lot of boxes we haven't emptied yet. You sure you didn't give it to someone?"

"Oh no...," she admonishes me for the mere thought. "I wouldn't have given Elvis away."

We keep opening boxes, an eye out for the King.

Mom is plugged in with access to cable TV in both rooms, lit to the ceiling with shaded lamps, small-appliance-readied, and kitchen-stuffed. High traffic lanes are cleared of jumbled cartons.

In drawers and on shelves, side by side, cornbread, biscuit mix, and Ajax powder, dusters, plastic bags of paper clips, and winter purses. No room for logic. Everything (not quite yet) in "a" place, even if not in "its" place. Still a few recalcitrant containers queue near their future abodes, awaiting permanent relocation.

All counter space is occupied: microwave, coffee pot, toaster, toaster oven, measuring cups, bananas, salt and peppershakers, trivets, paper towel holder. The stove, oven, refrigerator promise fried chicken, vegetable soup, grilled cheese sandwiches, roast beef and turkey but there's no room in this room to fry, bake, or cook.

Elsewhere, whatnots—complete with dust particles attached—continue to time travel, tethering my mother to houses that no longer exist and people long gone.

Mom casts a worried eye at the bookcase, searching for the King. I remind her there are still boxes to empty.

Later that day, my husband asks me what's up with this one cookbook. Is it an obsession with Presley? A fair question since my mother was an Elvis fan.

But there's more to it than that.

"The Elvis Presley Cookbook" ties together her two loves, the King and Rope, her husband who passed in 1996. Rope indulged every wish my mother ever had. He bought her nice jewelry, fanciful purses, any kitchen appliance she could imagine. She wanted to travel so he took her to Hawaii, and several times a year to Las Vegas where he gave her money to gamble and let her play bingo from sunup to sundown. In short, he spoiled and coddled her.

The one desire that he would not indulge was her obsession with cookbooks. As far as he was concerned, she had too many, more than she could possibly use, for cookbooks are not meant to be put on display but to be used. So, when Mom spied *The Elvis Presley Cookbook* in the Las

Vegas hotel lobby gift shop and announced that she wanted it, Rope said she didn't need it.

A few hours later, Mom snuck down to the giftshop and bought the cookbook on the sly. When they got home to Evansville, Rope handed Mom a paper bag. Inside was a copy of the King's cookbook, a young Elvis, gleaming white teeth and pomaded hair, on the cover. He had bought it for her "as a surprise."

Mom eventually snuck her secret copy out of the house and gave it to a friend. She never told Rope that she had already bought it.

Rope's gift of "The Elvis Presley Cookbook" came with more than celebrity value. It was a piece of Mom's life, a token between her and her husband.

Mission Challenge: Too many assets, no space. Identify and cull nonessential objects. Eliminate redundancies. Options: Pitch, Recycle, Donate.

As my mother moves in, I move out.

Seized by a dread of accumulated possessions, I return home to face our own clutter. Drawers overflow with the minutia of past lives. Closets gorge like fat moths on stale fabric. On wire hangers, like tobacco leaves hung to cure away from the sun, clothes from different decades stiffen and fade. I earmark those that have to go, bundle them into great stacks, stuff these into lawn bags. My husband drags the bags of clothing down to the curb for the next charity drive.

I cull old bank statements, bills, receipts for vinyl shades from a defunct company, emptying plastic storage containers that have sat on our upstairs chair in the hallway—as if the contents already knew that their presence must be transient. I sweep the rubbish into a thick plastic lawn bag. I tamp down regret and pitch whole cassette collections of 80s and 90s music into the same bag. I feel lighter as our trashcan bulges.

The vastness and weight of possessions no longer comforts me. Other bonds, bonds of affection and memory, tether me to my spot. No risk that I will float away, lost in the vacuum of space. The bric-a-brac of my life does not tell me who I am. These are things that we hold onto, to spite our forgetfulness, toys that gather dust on shelves that promise order but mock our futile efforts to stop time.

One more day, we think, of unpacking. We find several more cookbooks, but Elvis isn't among them. With each box we open, Mom gathers and nurtures her disappointment and frustration over the move from her two-bedroom apartment in Evansville to this two-college town in southern Minnesota where I work. The microwave display is screwy, but she can buy a new one. The computer doesn't work, but she only played Spider Bingo on it and never used the internet. But the missing cookbook? That is just one too many disappointments.

Then, looking for a missing electric roaster, we play a longshot. We drag out nonessential boxes that we had set aside in the initial days of unpacking. They had fit nicely at the back of the pantry. Then we forgot them. Until now. One box is big enough perhaps for the electric roaster. We pull it out and open the flaps.

Elvis smiles up at us. Mom smiles back.

The King is in the building!

Our Country 'Tis

we are no longer considered a full democracy
Heidi Schreck, "What the Constitution Means to Me."

I squint, blinded by the white
glare of a slanting ray
that gives no warmth.

America, we once took as ours
the name of an entire continent and the world let us. Our stars have dulled and
stripes remind us of the prison garb of old flicks.

The world turns and shakes
us off like fattened fleas from Zeus's hide into the saddle-tired lyrics of a
    country-western lament.

Our Commander in Chief
no longer counts our votes
to win the numbers game. Once our civic duty, we see
our right to have a say dwindle to a footnote on the frayed contract. Read the
    fine print
on the corporate constitution
we've been told to sign.

That slant ray from a dying
star stings the eyes—
morning collides with sunset.

On the Prairie

Those who came before me didn't belong
here. They had to slash their way
across unknown terrain from east to west,
irrigating their tracks with tears and blood.

Like malignant growths, they spread, took root deep among the bones of the
    displaced, pocking the land, excusing rape and pillage as divine destiny and
    human nature.

Waxing romantic, their progeny
swear over a merciless wind that siren words come strained through dry prairie
    reeds in a language half remembered, but still sung.

A Congress of Crows

We handed over the house and all our rights. For the crows had gathered in a
    congress of molting, black feathers and happy lice to hail the tyrant and the
    death of progress.

Caustic caws signaled the crowning feast. Fetid with power, beak filed, King
    Crow sank talons into the nation's fabric. Then, all
took flight, the state of the union in tow.

Bits of the common dropped by the wayside as the greedy birds cruised the sky.
What use amendments? What's the loss of a few rights?
It's the law of victory: the untaxed rich get a free ride.

Shredding, shedding our democracy into oil-inky skies, somewhere south of the
    border, crows caw and sing over cages, barbed wire fences, lost children's
    cries, seeding their dung, scattering woe on blighted wing.

With antebellum joy, Jefferson and Robert E. Lee sang "Dixie" while Detroit
    burned, the sick died, and Louisiana sank into the sea.
Columbus sailed his three yachts into New York harbor.
No one saw the clocks roll back or watched the crows soar.

The Groove

We can tell we're obsessed with a particular song when the needle on our record
    player scratches its way across worn vinyl grooves, jumping off path, forging
a short-cut through the song, skipping bars and words,
inserting a forced sonic gap

like the loss of a rotten front tooth.

Caught, as we often are, in an altered state induced by deafening decibels, sound
    waves pulsing like a supernova in a space-time continuum where the
    percussive beat sets the rhythm inside as well as outside our bodies, soaking
    through our porous white skin, rebounding within our hermetically sealed
    rooms, more than one of us, we solitary dancers
stumble in riotous, frenetic, jerky, idiosyncratic gyrations, stunned by the scritch-
    scratch
 disruption in our bliss,
miles from, and oblivious to, other beats and beatings.

It's no less disconcerting to hear Led Zeppelin's guitar riff on an endless loop,
   needle caught, like flotsam on a low tide, over and over the same trilling
   notes, the same lyrical phrase, echo after echo of John singing his plaintive
   Julia or blasting Revolution, or Paul stuck, like an entire generation, on
   Yesterday.
 Sound engineers, we wrestle with dust jams, polishing waxy grooves, flicking
microscopic dirt from diamond-hard needles. Readers of the labyrinth
of material sound, we resettle the balance and swing
the arm over the slick black landscape of the album
to the last path taken.
 After an initial scratch or plunk, holding our breath, we wait
to be carried off on the smooth voices of our musical gurus, the instrumental
   virtuosity of our heavy-metal gods, and the poetic verses and verities of our
   heart-stopping idols,
 to transcend the glitchy, botched stage of our adolescent lives,
the gritty acne of our hormonal skin, the aching loneliness
and stunning awkwardness of bodies in transit

to get unstuck from the worn tracks
of our grooved, tumultuous, 1960s lives,
to smooth away the nightly tally of deaths
in Vietnam, black bodies arms locked
on the bridge, students crumpled and bleeding
on college campuses, the drained faces
of Kennedys, King, and Malcom X,
cities on fire and people ablaze.

Thrones

Advice to a young king on the eve of his coronation

Heed this, your Highness:
straight-backed and rigid,
with a painful bas-relief design,
a throne is not made to be comfortable.

It is a cramped, three-sided office for one,
vulnerable in front. If my Lord brings a pillow
or a rump cushion,
The Privy Council could toss it out
(unauthorized props, unkingly)
or pull the lofty chair from beneath your royal derriere.

If the throne is gold, you can't see the precious stuff.
How can you see what you are squatting on?
Your Highness will discern a duplicitous simulation
of gold, however, in the eyes of footstools
when they are allowed to gaze up at your crowned head.
But if their shining reflections blind my Lord,
you will not see the sun rising
and sinking on your kingdom.

Should that happen, you, my Sovereign,
can't pocket all that gold,
unless it is dismantled, melted,
in which case you lose your balance,
and the gold will pocket you.

Lies

He threw the first plate accurately,
stood still and spun it.

He tossed another,
flipped up four more for height.
Soon he held fifteen at the end of long pole,
where they balanced,
holding their own,
a pattern.

The circus was silent.
We relaxed in the stands.

He was free to come
and go with his act,
no one saying a word.

Endgame Preacher

A traveling salesman of sorts,
he goes house to house,
knocking on mahogany doors,
pedaling Apocalypse.

Let in, he lingers,
stays long enough
for supper,
Hell and Damnation
at the end of a gleaming table,
brimstone for aperitif.

He expounds,
sweats scripture
over French food,
prefers instead a plain American diet.

Under unlit candles, appetites lost.
After dinner, the hosts
refuse to accept
The King James

Version of Himself.
So, he wedges abridged
pocket bibles,
secretively,
into the dark cracks
between leather sofa cushions.

For days the unconverted
can't relax, swear
something hard-edged
presses against them
from below, His Fiery
Word lodged there.

————Thank you, Northfield writers. Keep up the great work.————

After The Coup
Chile: September 11, 1973

Far away, in this warm house,
I read a hundred poems of Neruda.
Darkness covers the page:
Someone has knocked down a pole
On the gravel road.
My neighbors come with candles.
Their daughter tells me
She has seen a hummingbird
Flying in and out of my garden.
His song goes unheard:
It is too high for human ears.
They leave me alone here
Where the white heart of lettuce
Still grows, too near the president
Who turns over and laughs in his sleep
Unashamed.

for Pablo Neruda

February 22

Early morning, still dark
Outside my bedroom window.
Freezing rain drizzles down
Glazes trees and telephone wires
Windows, the grass, a homeless
Man's shiny blue tarp stretched
Between two abandoned cars
In a field in the middle of nowhere.
I hear my old friend nine years gone
Walking through the attic; all day
I see him pushing a cart
Full of books he's written on
How nature will save us
How our brains are not just wires
Attached to a machine
How our hearts were made
To be broken, to love and be loved,
Again and again. When I take
Your hand in mine, it is his hand
I'm taking; when I say your name
It is his. One day soon, the sun
Will rise over wildflowers blooming.
If you lie down on the earth
And listen carefully enough
You'll be able to hear a bluebell
 Ringing. …

for Paul Gruchow

Paul Gruchow

Medicine Mountain

t the summit of Medicine Mountain in the northern arc of the Big Horns, there is a construction in the shape of a wheel, built of stone. It is not clear who built it or why. Its history is shrouded because the people who established it as a sacred place are lost in unwritten time and the Crows who came after them, about the year of US independence, it is thought, never heard its story or were told it and forgot it. Nobody knows how, exactly, the circle of stones with twenty-eight spokes and seven cairns was intended to be used. Evidence grows, but not conclusively, that it was, at least in part, a celestial observatory. Astronomical evidence dates it as early as the twelfth century. Archeological evidence, however, dates it only to the late eighteenth century. If the archeological date is correct—it is based on tree-ring analysis on a piece of wood excavated from one of the cairns—it could not have been very old when the Crows first encountered it, and it is puzzling, therefore, that its story should have vanished. But vanish it has.

One thing is clear: It is a sacred place. To this day the ancient rites of the Native Americans are celebrated there, and it is generally agreed that worship of some kind has been practiced there for at least a couple of centuries. You would think it was a sacred place even if it were not marked as such, even if the wheel had not been built there. Some places are like that; they feel holy. You can't explain it. You can't point to evidence, cite data. Some things in the world wither and die in the face of too much scrutiny—poems and string quartets, for example—but this does not mean that they do not exist. Holy places are the same. They exist, but there is no use asking how or why or by what means. The summit of Medicine Mountain is one of them.

I had left my friend John behind—he had appointments to keep—and had gone on alone, headed farther west. I was not yet ready to take my leave of the mountains. Or perhaps they had not yet released me. So I approached the summit of Medicine Mountain alone one morning. It was gray and windy, raw, on the mountaintop. In the west, dark clouds growled menacingly. They hid the distant ranges, the Tetons, the Absarokas, the Beartooths,

My aloneness traveled with me that morning like a companion. It walked beside me, benign and peaceful, calming me and affirming my silence. I had not yet spoken a single word that day to any other human being, and I was glad, now that I approached Medicine Mountain, to be under no obligation to speak, to exclaim, to take account of any presence save that of the mountain.

All holy places command us, if only for a little while, to keep silence. I suppose that to be speechless is to go back to the beginning of things, back to our own individual beginnings when we knew nothing but the cry for help. And back to the voiceless beginning of life on earth when the water of the primordial soup churned and the winds raged, and nothing heard or saw. In speechlessness begins our awe for life.

The mountains in the vicinity of the wheel are of a different sort than the ones I had been walking in. They are lower—about ten thousand feet in elevation—rounder, softer. The hard gray granite has given way to a soft yellow limestone, and the mountainsides are green in summer, not only with pines but with gentle and aromatic cedars. In the moist crevices of the green valleys, groves of silvery aspens grow. The tops of the mountains are bald, like the heads of old men. They are covered not with boulders but with a fuzz of wispy grass, like the last hairs of men growing bald. They have old-mountain names: Bald Mountain, Sheep Mountain, Medicine Mountain.

It is a region of small caves. The entrance to one of them lies scarcely a hundred yards from the wheel. It is a place to hide and in which things are hidden.

At the same time, it embraces three visible worlds. To the west, you can look a mile down into the basin below. The Big Horn River winds through it like a piece of string, and you can see towns the size of toys. It is high enough so that you feel diminished before the world, and this is good. This feeling of diminishment is the beginning of reverence for life. Still, the face of the mountain falls precipitously in a sheer limestone cliff just beyond the upper edge of the wheel. High as you are, you have the sensation that it would be only a short leap into the lap of the plains. You imagine that you might stretch out your arms and take flight like an eagle and soar to a resting place in the sagebrush. Here you belong simultaneously to the mountains and to the plains, and this is good. You feel empowered with choices, and in such empowerment is the beginning of joy for life. Yet the great dome of the sky rises all around you. Beyond the mountains and the plains stretches the third world, the unimaginable world of the universe. You feel the mysterious void, and this, too, is good. In mystery begins thankfulness for life.

I approach the wire fence that encircles the medicine wheel, saddened by the reminder that even in such places we somehow manage to act as if nothing were sacred.

I walked around and around the wheel, very slowly, pausing to consider it from each new angle. I noted the daisies blooming in the grass, the pika that fled from one of the cairns as I approached, the ladybugs soaking up the warmth of a stone, the charred remains of some recent ceremonial fire. It was a monument, like all monuments. What distinguished it, I thought, was the purity of its setting, so spare and austere, so high and silent, so grandly inclusive of sky and plains and mountains, a place conjoining the whole world of the people who came here to worship.

The Bighorn medicine wheel is one of forty or fifty similar structures so far discovered on the northern Great Plains. It is the largest and best known of these, a roughly circular pattern of stones, about eighty-two feet in diameter, laid out on the surface of the ground. At the center of the circles lies a cairn in the shape of a broken doughnut, about ten feet around, and from it twenty-eight lines of stones, irregularly placed, radiate out to the rim. There are six further cairns here and there along the rim, five of them situated on the circle and the sixth a few feet outside it. Except for the central cairn the construction is modest in scale, there being generally no more than one or two courses of stones, and the stones being roughly the size of footballs.

The first White person to see the site was probably a gold prospector from nearby Bald Mountain City, a mining camp of the 1880s, which was succeeded in the 1890s by the boom town of Fortunatus. Rumor had it that the Indians knew of a fabulous lode of gold somewhere on or near Big Baldy, as the mountain was called. But nobody ever found it. "Money flowed freely," the Federal Writers Project guide to Wyoming reports dryly, "and everyone prospered but the miners and investors."

By 1895 the first printed reference to the wheel had appeared in *Field and Stream* in an account of a hunting expedition, the author likening it to the "Calendar Sone of Old Mexico," a guess more accurate than any to appear for the next eighty years if current scholarship is correct.

The first scholarly examination of the site was undertaken in 1902 by S.C. Simms of the Field Columbian Museum. Simms, an anthropologist, questioned Crow tribal leaders about it. None had actually seen the site, but a few of them had heard of it from their father. They told him it was an ancient holy place but professed not to know its origins, saying only that it was made "by people who had no iron." There was a bleached buffalo skull at the sight when Simms visited it, near the center cairn facing east toward the rising sun.

The wheel was photographed in 1902 and 1915 and mapped in 1917. These records have satisfied subsequent investigators that the sight is authentic and that it has not been significantly altered since.

In 1922 anthropologist George Bird Grinnell noted the similarity of the wheel to the floor plan of the Sun Dance lodges of the Plains Indians and suggested that it was representation of such a lodge, built, perhaps a by the Cheyenne.

A thorough, not to say persnickety, assessment of the site was undertaken in 1958 by the Wyoming Archeological Society under the direction of Don Grey. (Persnickety: the construction, Grey argued, should not be called a medicine wheel because it is not literally a wheel, for one thing; and for another, because the definition of a medicine wheel then in academic vogue prescribed something with spokes radiating from a central point, and in this case, the spokes radiate from the outside wall of the center cairn, not from the middle of it. Nevertheless, he said, he might *call* it a medicine wheel, given historical precedent, so long as a medicine wheel was understood to be "a compound polarogram constructed upon the earth in loose stone, wood, or earth." I am trying not to giggle.) The investigators made a new map of the wheel and excavated down to bedrock all the cairns and about a third of the spaces between the twenty-eight spokes in the wheel. The excavations produced nothing particularly revealing: a few stone artifacts, a few pottery shards, some bone fragments, and nine beads. The central cairn yielded a piece of buffalo bone and the information that a two-foot-deep pit had been dug into the limestone bedrock there. In one of the outer cairns, wedged into the stones, the archeologists found a piece of tree limb. An analysis of its rings suggested that it dated from approximately 1760. Therefore, Grey concluded, the site could be no more than about two hundred years old.

This conclusion stood until 1974 when astronomer, John A. Eddy, proposed an entirely new way of looking at the site. In a report published in *Science*, Eddy suggested that the real significance of the medicine wheel had been missed because earlier investigators had concentrated on the wheel and its rims. In fact, he said, the importance of the structure lies in its cairns.

Eddy guessed that the cairns were markers for astronomical observations of some sort. He set out to test this hypothesis in 1972 and 1973. An examination of the site persuaded him that the observations had to be connected to the summer solstice since it is snowbound and generally inaccessible during the winter solstice. Indeed, shortly before the summer solstice in 1972, boot-deep snow fell there, and four days before the solstice in 1973 a late storm halted traffic on a nearby highway. But these snows demonstrated the practicality of the site. While the storms left the mountainsides at lower elevations deeply covered in snow, winds swept the medicine wheel site bare within two or three days. Still, Eddy conceded, "the choice of a cold and arduously reached mountaintop in preference to the equally usable nearby plains must be justified on other grounds—possibly mystical or purely aesthetic."

Eddy found confirmation of his hypothesis on that cold solstice day in 1972. A sighting from the cairn he labeled E through the center cairn marked the solstice sunrise, and a sighting for the cairn he labeled C through the center cairn marked the solstice sunset, not exactly, but close enough. The statistical odds, he calculated, that any of the two cairns placed by chance would align with the solstice sunrise and sunset are about one in four thousand.

Two questions remained. How might the other four cairns have been used? And at what time in history would the marking have been exact?

As for the cairns, Eddy found answers for three of them. For cairn F, the largest of the peripheral markers, the builders could have sighted the star Aldebaran rising over cairn A; Rigel over cairn B; and Sirius over the center cairn. These happen to be the three brightest morning stars rising near the path of the sun in the summer sky over the Big Horns. And they would have been important stars to someone using celestial sightings to mark the calendar.

Although it is not true now, in earlier centuries Aldebaran made its first rising with the sun just before the summer solstice. Its appearance would have been important because the sun moves rather slowly along the horizon at the time of the solstice, making it difficult to mark its occurrence exactly. But the first yearly rising of a star is rather easy for a practiced observer to pinpoint to within two or three days. So the first appearance of Aldebaran would have signaled quite precisely the solstice day.

In the centuries when Aldebaran served to mark the solstice, furthermore, Rigel made its first yearly appearance exactly one lunar month later, and Sirius first appeared exactly one lunar month after that. (I mean lunar month here in the sense that the Indians did, as including only the twenty-eight days in each synodic month when the moon is visible.) With the first rising of Sirius, in other words, the two high summer months of the alpine season would have passed, and seeing it, nomadic hunters in the mountains would have known that it was time to pack up and head back to the plains for the winter. Probably they made their descent along the well-marked travois trail that passes within easy distance of the medicine wheel.

As for dating when the wheel might have been constructed, the same difficulties arise as in deciding when the precise day of the solstice has occurred. But, again, these difficulties are not present with respect to Aldebaran. Eddy calculated that the Aldebaran alignment could have been made any time from about 1500 to about 1900. The most likely guess, he said, is that cairn F was built about 1700.

Since then another astronomer, Jack Robinson, has proposed a possible use for cairn D, the one that stumped Eddy. A sighting from cairn F through cairn D, Robinson proposed, would have been useful from about 1050 to 1450 in locating the rising with the sun of another very bright morning star, Fomalhaut, which would have made its first appearance one lunar month before the summer solstice, it would have been, then, one more observation useful in pinpointing accurately the time of the solstice, If Robinson is correct, obviously, the wheel would considerably predate 1700, an idea, I think, that Eddy would not resist. In fact, Eddy was the first scholar to suggest that the medicine lodges of the Plains Indians may have been patterned after the medicine wheels and not, as is usually presumes, the other way around.

Were the Plains Indians good enough astronomers to make all of this credible? "The answer is surely yes," Eddy wrote, "There should be little doubt that any people who lived by the sun would intimately know the dawn, and that any who lived at the mercy of the seasons would know as well the solstices."

There remains the matter of the twenty-eight spokes and the ring of stones that connects them. The ring might be simply ornamental, and the spokes have one obvious use in calendar keeping. They could have been markers for the days of the lunar month.

Recently anthropologist Robert L. Hall suggested that all of the speculation about the wheel may be right, that it is *both* a representation of a medicine lodge and an observatory, and that the site has significance even beyond these interpretations.

The twenty-eight spokes have both practical and ritual connections. Twenty-eight, for example, is the number of days in a month as the Plains Indians counted them. Each of these days had a particular symbolic significance, Black Elk, a holy man of the Oglala Sioux, explained:

> …two of the days represent the Great Spirit; two are for the Mother Earth; four are for the four winds; one is for the Spotted Eagle; one for the sun; and one for the moon; one is for the morning star; and four are for the four ages; seven are for our seven great rites; one is for the buffalo; one is for the fire; one is for the water; one is for the rock; and finally one is for the two-legged people. If you add these days up you will see that they come to twenty-eight.

Hence the twenty-eight poles in a ceremonial lodge. Again, the buffalo has twenty-eight ribs, upon which the Plains Indian depended for their lives. The number of these ribs was not something that might have escaped their notice. Again, in Plains culture, the sacred numbers were four and seven. Four for the winds, the ages, the quarters of the earth, the seasons. Seven for the seven days, the seven rites, the seven cardinal directions (north, south, east, west, up, down, and here). And, of course, the product of the sacred numbers is twenty-eight. Even if the spokes in the wheel were merely ornamental, there would have been twenty-eight of them, automatically, instinctively, even as an orator in our own culture rises in our debate to make three points.

What particularly attracted Hall's attention, however, was not the spokes or the rim of the wheel but the shape of its cairns. They are all roughly round, but each has an opening, and the openings all appear to be placed at random. The cairns do not mark the directions, and they do not open in ways consistent with their uses as guides to celestial observation. What could they mean?

To Hall, the cairns looked keyhole-shaped, reminiscent to him of similar shapes in the ritual construction of other Native American cultures. They reminded him of a shrine on Chicoma Mountain in New Mexico, the earth alters of the Omaha, the keyhole-shaped prayer symbol of the Pawnees, the Cahokia woodhenges at the site of the great pre-Columbian agricultural city east of St. Louis on the Mississippi River flood plain.

And the wheel in its totality was suggestive not only of Pawnee earth lodges, and of Cheyenne tipi encampments. It reminded Hall, as well, of the netted hoops of the Piegan Indians of Alberta, Canada, and of those used in the hoop and pole games of the Plains Indians.

These are two sets of images with the same implications. The keyhole images, Hall contends, are all variations on the structure that the Pueblo called the earth navel. He quotes Alfonso Ortiz, a Pueblo by birth and an anthropologist by training, on the significance of the earth navel: "It functions as a sacred center in two respects. First, it is the point at which one may communicate with the spiritual underworld, and second, it serves to gather them, through the open end, to the Tewa villages." In the village where Ortiz was born, further, the earth navel was the site of an annual ceremony of renewal. At the beginning of the growing season, seeds from all the food plants important to the village were planted in the earth navel in a ritual intended each year to reawaken nature.

The netted hoop images, on the other hand, recall the spiderweb, a natural trap with meaning in the rituals of many Indian nations. The spiderweb, the Indians noted, caught not only prey for the spider, but also moisture because the dewdrops condensed on it, and the sun itself, trapped in the drops of dew. So it symbolized the rain and the sunshine of the annual rebirth of the earth in spring. It was also used as a symbol in the buffalo fertility rites of the Plains Indians.

A ritual game was played with a netted hoop and pole, in which the pole represented the buffalo bull and the hoop the cow, and the penetration of the hoop by the pole was a metaphor for fertilization.

It is consistent with what we know about Indian culture, Hall argues, to suppose that the wheel on Medicine Mountain had a variety of uses. Perhaps it sustained the observations necessary to determine the coming of the summer solstice when the blessings of the sun were thought to be most powerful. Perhaps it had connections with the Sun Dance rituals, which were meant to honor dead chiefs. But it is also likely, he says, that the wheel was a world center, an earth navel, for the nations occupying that region. If so, the cairns would be properly understood as having both the passive purpose of marking celestial phenomena and the active purpose of catching the blessing of the earth and directing them to the nations that worshipped there. Their openings, in this case, would be seen not as random but as pointing to the home grounds of the tribes. And the spokes and rim of the wheel would be understood as recalling not only the medicine lodges but also the webs of the fertility rites.

The argument appeals to me, in part because the site of the Bighorn medicine wheel is so spectacularly well suited to such a grand purpose. From it one really does feel connected with every part of a vast homeland. But it is an argument that no one, least of all me, is in a position to settle now. What is not written down is eventually lost. The world that the wheel represents has vanished. We can imagine it, well or badly, but we can never know it.

Perhaps, therefore, all this is moot. But I think not. I think two things, on reflection, about my visit there. I am, for one thing, touched by the sentence with which Dr. Eddy's pathbreaking report ends. "With the encroachment of a white civilization on the northern plains in the 19th century," he wrote, "the Indian's requirement for a natural calendar could have vanished, taking with it certain astronomical traditions." *Taking with it certain astronomical traditions.* I think of all that some prehistoric peoples knew about the stars, and of all that most of us now don't know about them. It reminds me that a culture can get a lot more urbane without growing one iota richer. And I think of Hall's argument. *It would be consistent with what we know about Indian culture to suppose that its artifacts had both practical and spiritual significance.* That, I think, is an argument that no anthropologist a millennium hence will ever be moved to make about us. Let it be said: We knew the difference between the spiritual and the practical. And let the question ring:'And what good did knowing it ever do us.

Look for these new releases this Fall, 2022.

Four Arbitrary Rules of Illiberal Democracy

One: Undermine Democracy at the Polls by Undermining the Polls.

In 1925, during Germany's Great Depression, former Field Marshal Paul von Hindenburg took the reins of government to become only the second President in the young democratic republic's post-WWI history. Two and a half years earlier, a German court had sent Adolf Hitler to prison for high treason for his role in a failed coup d'état at the Reichstag. After serving barely nine months of his five-year sentence, Hitler left prison a man free to continue where he had left off.

Hindenburg's coalition government crumpled in 1930 under pressure from the right, primarily exerted by the Nazis. In 1932, three million German's petitioned Hindenburg to run for a second term to stop Hitler from gaining any more popularity and power. With democracy already on the ropes, Hindenburg, at age eighty-four, reluctantly agreed to run again that March. Hitler's Nazi Party received nearly one-third of the votes cast, sending the election to a second round in April. Hindenburg won a majority. After the victory, his greatest challenge was both economic and political: fix the economy and end galloping inflation; and stand between what remained of the late Weimer period's illiberal democracy and Adolf Hitler's bellicose despotism.

Hindenburg's two successive picks for chancellor both failed on the economy. His second pick only lasted a couple of days, but Franz von Papen would later become Hitler's vice chancellor. Hindenburg disbanded the *Reichstag* and called for yet another election on July 31, 1932.

Third time was the charm for the Nazis. They did not win a majority but gained a solid plurality at 41 percent. In an illiberal turn of the democratic screw, Hitler seized enough power that the Weimar President had no choice but to try and out maneuver Hitler by appointing him chancellor.

In January 1933, the President of the Reich sacrificed the chancellorship to Hitler, hoping the Reichstag could swap power in exchange for a share of Hitler's popularity. Hindenburg and his coattail counselors desperately wanted to believe that the reins of power would tame Hitler and moderate his unpredictable behavior until such a time the Nazi chancellor's supporters realized that Hitler too proved unable to fix the shattered economy; then the Reichstag could dismiss him. But in Hitler's first year as chancellor, January to December 1933, unemployment fell from forty-four to thirteen percent. Together with other legally destructive moves, Hitler succeeded in obliterating what remained of democracy.

In the six-year period between taking over as chancellor in 1933 and the start of WWII in 1939, Hitler built his fearsome war, propaganda, and concentration-death machines. In '34, he declared himself *Fürer*. Hitler and the Nazis took their time perfecting inhumanity on their own people. The *Fürer* flattened the Weimar democratic experiment. Propaganda minister Joseph Goebbels honed his misinformation skills and developed the infrastructure to deliver racist, white supremacist values to the German people. Goebbels' trampled the once constitutionally free press. Political opposition, much of it coming from what remained of the media, went into hiding.

Before the Nazi's illiberal democratic chrysalis exploded into a monstrous dictatorship, the Weimar Republic had become a haven for a dynamic, pluralistic media, including small and large commercial presses. Ruhr industrial interests opposed to the rise of Hitler provided loans to these presses and news wire services, hoping to manipulate public opinion in favor of Hindenburg's Second Reich.

Journalists reported at their peril, however, and anti-Nazi activists were jailed. The Third Reich constructed its first concentration camp at Dachau. Weimar Germany had been a safe gathering center for LGBTQ people. Under Hitler, they were rounded up, along with the Roma; the community of intellectuals, artists, unionists, and socialists considered impure and dangerous. German Jews were constrained in their private and public lives by more than four hundred edicts and regulations.

The renowned innovation and artistic culture that had captured the eye of the creative world during the Weimar period ended abruptly. Germans with the means to emigrate, many of them Jewish, did so. Bauhaus artists led by the renowned architect, Walter Gropius, German Expressionist painters, sculptors and filmmakers—Marlene Dietrich starring as Lola in Josef von Sternberg's "The Blue Angel"—Berthold Brecht whose plays included "Three Penny Opera," with Lotte Lenya singing, and "Mother Courage and Her Children," written in 1939 about the Hundred Years War in reaction to the invasion of Poland and the official start of WWII, were among those who left.

Illiberal democracy is nothing to play with, and too often, believers in orthodox democracy do just that, voting themselves into oblivion on the notion that *fair is fair.* (Fair is not always fair.)

I want to be clear about raising the specter of Hitler and the genocidal Nazis in the Age of Trump World and the Republican ass-kissers clinging to the cuff of his trousers. I have invoked Hitler and his Nazi Party only to illustrate the similarities between the fall of the Weimar Republic, and how populist demagogues, wherever they appear, can stress illiberal democratic societies to the point of failure.

Two: Lease the Loyalty of Your Voters.

I arrived in Libreville, Gabon, on Africa's West Coast, in 1983, a US Peace Corps volunteer. Gabon began pretending to be a democracy December 1968 under the leadership of autocrat and eventual natural resources magnate, Omar Bongo. Bongo hailed from his eponymous birth village of Bongoville, *Haute Ogooué* Province, Gabon.

Peace Corps posted my wife Beth and I in the Haute Ogooué on *le Plateau Batéké.* Our consolidated village, *Ali-ga,* named after a mandated re-grouping of neighboring villages, to bring rural Gabonese to designated routes, was situated not far as the crow flies from Bongoville. But in fact, a couple of hours wrestling a Land Cruiser through deep rivers of white sand, characteristic of the Plateau, to the paved road, only brought you within thirty minutes of Bongoville.

Omar Bongo took over for his autocratic predecessor in 1967 and established the *Parti Democratique Gabonese* in March 1968. All citizens were invited to join the single-party realm. According to Wikipedia, this example of illiberal democracy is known as a Unitary Dominant-Party Presidential Republic. There are at least sixty de facto single-party presidential and provincial (state) illiberal democratic systems operating in the world today. These national and provincial governments increase the opportunities for restricting voter rights, dominating minority rule, allowing corruption from top to bottom, as well as tyranny of both the majority and the minority, which can lead to dysfunctional parliaments, social apartheid, racial and ethnic segregation, lack of access to healthcare, to polls, to social justice, to civil rights, etcetera.

President Bongo held Gabon's first single-party election in 1973. Running unopposed, he ended up with 96.6 percent of the vote. Eligible voters reelected him again in 1977 and 1980.

Bona fide liberal democracy began to undermine Bongo's authoritarian one-party system, however, leading up to and following the election of 1985. In 1990, Bongo's opponents forced him to dissolve one-party rule. Increasingly tighter races pitted Bongo against skilled, vocal candidates from a raft of newly formed parties. But despite multi-party elections, Bongo managed to hang onto parliament and the presidency through elections in 1993, 1998, 2001, and 2005, shortly before his death.

I remember voting in the 1985 election, a participant in choosing the head of state in a foreign country. Illiberal democracy, not a coup.

There had been no campaign as far as I knew. Though plenty of cash from le Président flowed throughout the Haute Ogooué into remote Plateau villages and all around the country through local units of government. One morning, the inhabitants of Ali-ga greeted me with the enthusiasm and energy usually reserved for holidays. Community pride seemed awfully high; it was Election Day!

Chef André, whose French was about as good as my Batéké, repeated through Bruno, one of my workers on the Peace Corps school we were building, *« Monsieur Tomas, Votez! »*

I laughed. "I can't vote in your election."

"You live in Ali-ga, monsieur Tomas; you must vote."

So, I walked through dirty sand to the village *buvette* that served as the polling place. Several people sat on bamboo stools smoking cigarettes rolled from a student's notebook paper containing village tobacco and herbs harvested in the forest. They were drinking early, even for Ali-ga. I greeted everybody then checked a box on a mimeographed square of grainy, torn paper next to the name of Président Omar Bongo.

The aluminum *tôle* roofed bar was always scorching during daylight. I hurried to leave. Outside, Chef André and Bruno waited, grinning. André somberly uncrumpled a one-thousand CFA note; CFA was the French-backed currency used at the time by France's former colonies.

« C'est quoi ça ? »

« C'est mille francs, Tomas. Vous avez voté. C'est pour vous. »

It was then, and it is now, mind-bending. Mille francs, the price of one of those lukewarm big fat brown bottles of state subsidized beer, given in exchange for bringing home the 99.97 percent vote for the perennial incumbent and leader of Gabon's Unitary Dominant-Party Presidential Republic. 1985 would be the last time el Hadj Omar Bongo would be able to pay for universal fealty. Voters may or may not have continued to receive gratuities to vote for one candidate or another, but their benefactor would have to come from one of seventeen parties registered to run for the presidential and parliamentary

election of 1990 and all the illiberal democratic elections to follow.

Three: Arrogance. Brutality. Kleptocracy. Uncertainty.

I am still fascinated by the vote I so carelessly cast for Bongo in 1985, and more introspective about its irony as time passes and I better understand the short lifespans of governments. My interest in illiberal democracy started in Gabon and only grew when I went to work for the US Agency for International Development in Burundi, Rwanda, Tanzania, and the Democratic Republic of the Congo (DRC), known back in the day as *le Zaïre*, ruled for thirty-two years by Mobutu Sese Seko.

How does someone so autocratic as Mobutu gain power? Congo's only democratic election produced Patrice Lumumba after all. There was turmoil following Congolese independence in 1960. Chaos can be a fertile sea for despots. There were multiple breakaway movements, especially the secession of mineral-rich Katanga; Mobutu ousting Congo's prime minister, Patrice Lumumba, and Lumumba's assassination; five years of uneven rule by President Joseph Kasavubu, culminating in civil war against *Simba* rebels. Once the dust finally settled, Mobutu, with the support of the CIA and former colonial governments, led a second coup, deposing and jailing Kasavubu on *Vingt-quatre novembre*, declaring himself head of state and leader of the only political party permitted henceforth, *le Mouvement Populaire de la République*.

By many accounts, young Mobutu was pragmatic, honest in word and deed, handsome, charismatic, and likable. I have often wondered, what changed him? By the time I got to Zaïre in 1988, he was regarded by both Zaïrians and expatriates to be entrenched in ruthless tyranny and self-serving kleptocracy. Despite Zaïre's enormous natural resource wealth, the country was perennially poor, and always looking for foreign aid programs to tend to its citizens' most basic needs. (Just not their sociopolitical needs.) Mobutu and his Rolodex of government officials saw to it that anyone who stepped over the line, colored outside the lines, or refused to get back in line would be dealt with, and harshly, if required.

Maybe handing over Patrice Lumumba to be viciously assassinated turned Mobutu heartless. Lumumba was no saint. At independence, he used Russian aircraft to divide loyalties among his international allies, and to ferry his Army to the capitol of the secessionist Kasai province, Bakwanga, (Mbuji-Mai today). On orders from Lumumba, soldiers crossed the line from putting down a rebellion to attempting genocide of the Luba tribe. Or was it the deceitfully gruesome murder of Pierre Mulele, a Maoist separatist leader of the Simbas, that twisted Mobutu? He lured Mulele from exile with a promise of amnesty. When Mulele arrived in Kinshasa, Mobutu had him tortured, his eyes and genitals gouged and torn out, his limbs hacked off, all of this while he was alive. Then he was thrown into the Congo River.

At some point during his early years of despotism, Mobutu realized one of the foremost tenets of single-party loyalty was fear, fear inculcated through brutality. Unthinkable violence and the uncertainty created by false benevolence, a dreadful Yin-Yang of ambiguity, oppressed the general population and government officials for twenty-five years. Mobutu cultivated a signature style of doubt in government that kept the nation, its appointed leadership, the collective of often restive tribes, and forty-million individuals on their toes. It was known as *Remaniement*, a reorganization of department heads from the prime minister, minister of the interior, head of the central bank and the Army, all the way down to provincial governors and village administrators. By 1991, Mobutu had engineered no fewer than thirty-three Remaniements.

In response to inflation, which proved to be another enduring problem for Mobutu—steady erosion of the zaïre—*le Guide* as he was known, went to his old print more money playbook, adding a tweak. Before devaluing the zaïre, money changers and anyone carrying cash to pay for dinner, for example, carried it in large paper sacks full of often filthy one-thousand z-notes, with a couple five or ten thousand z's thrown in, to pay for a meal that might cost 100,000-200,000 zaïres. To fix the problem, Mobutu ordered the mint to print a one million-z note. I have one framed because I still think it's absurd. Not so the military. When Mobutu ordered his troops to be paid with million z-notes, his military went ballistic and rioted for a week, causing one to two thousand deaths. The mutiny signaled the beginning of a slow-motion end of the regime of the notorious "warrior who knows no defeat because of his endurance and inflexible will and is all powerful, leaving fire in his wake as he goes from conquest to conquest," or some such variant of the name *Mobutu Sese Seko Kuku Ngbendu Wa Za Banga* he conferred upon himself.

He named the currency early on when he introduced *Authenticité* regulations: changing the name of country, mighty river, and currency to Zaïre; and creating a dress code for government elites, the *abacost,* a contracted form for the inauthentic French phrase, *à bas le costume,* meaning down with western suits and ties. He also renamed towns, provinces, natural features—cities like Bakwanga became Mbuji-Mai, Elizabethville became Lubumbashi, Stanleyville became Kisangani; Katanga Province became Shaba Province; Stanley Pool in the Congo River was renamed Malebo Pool. He renamed government titles, like minister, citizen even, as a form of address, to *Commissaire d'état, Commissaire Régionale,* and *Citoyen.* Mobutu's audacious arrogance stoked fear, uncertainty, and suffering.

Four: Illiberal Democracy **is** *Democracy.*

Piss around perverting democratic principles, rearranging the titanic deck chairs of our common good, making all the voyagers in a painted boat upon a painted ocean of selfish dreams nervous; do not be surprised if the sleeping albatross whose tail you have disturbed wakes up and slaps you and your fellow travelers, your allies, and your enemies a million ways to shitless.

This has been a major problem since the human species first organized itself: the annihilation of everything a society works for. We know that the nature of our planet is productive and destructive; there's no reason to think that humans are any different from the grand system that provides for and endangers our futures.

Just because your party or your candidate loses does not mean democracy has failed you or the role you have played by participating. Losing and winning on the slippery iceberg of collective ideas is democracy's greatest strength. Not that democracy isn't flawed. Consider Joe Manchin, a two term Democratic Senator from West Virginia. Manchin's gratitude to the fossil fuel industry is worthy of an ethics probe. Remember, industry is synonymous with production, not destruction. Manchin refuses to vote for the Biden administration's climate change legislation after months of negotiations, dooming a planned reduction in greenhouse gas emissions chiefly caused by fossil fuel use. In the absence of already tardy action to mitigate climate change, the painted boat we all travel on could spontaneously combust or founder in a terminal cosmological deluge.

Manchin no longer holds the White House climate change team hostage to his vote; negotiations collapsed; Manchin has symbolically murdered the experts in a contemptuous display of illiberal democracy. His motivations I would guess are politics and power; he is beholden to the fossil fuel industry, and he is in a position to assert control over the Senate, shoving Senate Majority Leader Chuck Schumer toward

irrelevancy. Rules and party be damned. Twice legally elected to the Senate, Manchin has intentionally created uncertainty for the Biden administration almost from its inception just two weeks after the January 6, 2021, insurrection at the US Capitol.[12]

My point is, there is no distance between Illiberal Democracy and Democracy. They are conceptual ambiguities on a circular spectrum, with the most liberally orthodox on one end of the scale and the most illiberally unorthodox on the other.

Sinister, illiberal democracy appears flawed but still democratic, before exhausting the usefulness of electoral guile entirely and another nationalist autocrat appears on top of the pile calling the shots.

It's an old saw, but never truer than today: Democracy is only as strong as its voters. Without an engaged collective of voters seeking Truth in Government—no matter your party—a democracy weakened toward the illiberal, might yield to its alternatives. Rally your party faithful, open the big tent and invite newcomers, first time voters; expand the electorate and vote for Democracy before someone shows up with a mob and capsizes your imaginary ship of state.

---

[12] Just as we're ready to drag this issue onto the launch pad, Senate Majority Leader Chuck Schumer and West Virginia Democrat Joe Manchin reached a "climate deal" worth $369 billion. That's great news, even greater if Democrats overcome GOP opposition and pass the bill— funds to fight climate change, and some to allow Medicare to negotiate drug prices with pharmaceutical companies, among other provisions.

But I'm going to stand by what I said about Manchin creating uncertainty for President Biden's plans, making it

appear, too often, that he, Manchin, is the final arbiter of administration policy.

Nothing Joe Manchin has done in the Senate appears illegal, though his behavior has that fishy smell sometimes of an unethical soup kitchen, or a sausage factory that technically bans ludicrous earmarks for the home district.

On either side of where they overlap on the spectrum, illiberal and liberal democracy in the US often appears to be a distinction without any real difference.

Contributors

M. Seth Yorra: Holds doctorates in law and psychoanalysis; masters in playwriting and psychoanalysis; bachelor in German Dramatic Literature, maintains small practices in psychoanalysis and law, and writes play after play. He notes that "occasionally one is produced." Seth lives in Rockport, Massachusetts.

Anthony S. Heck: An attorney, he devotes more time toward his passion for creative writing. He previously held the position of senior technical editor for the *New England Journal on Criminal and Civil Confinement*. He resides in New York, New York, with his partner and fluffy dog.

Ellen Thompson: Is a pseudonym for Yelena Teleshova of West Palm Beach, Florida. She has written poetry for fifteen years, and is the author of the poetry collection, "Love's Olympus."

Mercury-Marvin Sunderland: (he/him) is a transgender autistic gay man with borderline personality disorder. He's from Seattle and currently attends the Evergreen State College His poems have previous appeared in University of Amsterdam's *Writer's Block*, University of British Columbia's *Decomp*, UC Davis's *Open Ceilings*, UC Riverside's *Santa Ana River Review*, and UC Santa Barbara's *Spectrum*. His lifelong dream is to become the most banned author in human history.

Sean Murphy: writes plays about belonging, kindness and surviving trauma. When he is not writing plays, he is working in homeless services or adopting cats out of alleys. In past lives Mr. Murphy has been a songwriter, a stagehand, a high school dropout, a butterfly chaser, a rejection slip collector, a workers' rights activist, a blue-collar bon vivant and a legal services attorney. *Memory is a Thief* was selected in a national competition and staged in Asheville, North Carolina, for the 2021 Magnetic Theater One Act Play Festival.

Emilio DeGrazia: Award winning author of many novels, collections of poetry and essays, he lives with his wife Monica in Winona. His most recent collection, "What Trees Know," Nodin Press, 2020.

Don Kropp: Is a former Deputy Probation Officer, teacher and social writer. At eighty-eight years, he is a tired social writer with considerable life experience. Don no longer believes English editors are familiar with social history; that many are bamboozled, along with our under-informed citizenry.

Ken McCullough: Has received numerous awards for his poetry including the Academy of American Poets Award, a National Endowment for the Arts Fellowship, a Pablo Neruda Award, a Galway Kinnell Poetry Prize. Ken's most recent books include "Crossings: The Poets Laureate of Winona, Minnesota" (Shipwreckt Books, 2021), which won a Minnesota Book Awards silver medal for best anthology; and the collection, "Dark Star" (Red Dragonfly Press 2017). He has taught at Montana State University, the University of Iowa, Saint Mary's University of Minnesota, Viterbo University, UW-La Crosse and Winona State University. He lives in Winona with his wife, playwright Lynn Nankivil.

Dan Butterfass: Holds an MFA in Creative Writing from Vermont College of Fine Arts and a BA in English Literature from Carleton College. Dan taught English at Rochester Community and Technical College. His collection "Aerie" will be released this Fall by Up On Big Rock Poetry Series.

Elizabeth Oness: Writer & musician, lives on a biodynamic farm in Southeast Minnesota. Her poems and stories have appeared in *The Georgia Review, The Gettysburg Review, Glimmer Train, The Hudson Review, The Tahoma Literary Review*, and other magazines. Her stories have received an O. Henry Prize, a Nelson Algren Award, and the Crazyhorse Fiction Prize. Her books include "Articles of Faith, "Departures," "Twelve Rivers of the Body," "Fallibility." and "Leaving Milan."

David Sapp: A writer, artist and professor, lives along the southern shore of Lake Erie in North America. A Pushcart nominee, he was awarded an Ohio Arts Council Individual Excellence grant and an Akron Soul Train fellowship for poetry. His poems appear widely in the United States, Canada and the United Kingdom. Publications include articles in the *Journal of Creative Behavior*, chapbooks "Close to Home" and "Two Buddha," and a novel, "Flying Over Erie."

Gerald Lynch: Born in Monaghan, Ireland, Gerald grew up in Canada. He is the author of the novels, "The Dying Detective," "Omphalos," and "Missing Children" (Signature Editions, 2020, 2017). Working as a Professor at the University of Ottawa, in 2017 Gerald coedited "Miraculous Art: Critical Essays," by Alice Munro. He is the recipient of a few awards, including the gold award for short fiction in Canada's National Magazine Awards.

C. Mikal Oness: Is the author of "Oracle Bones," winner of the Lewis & Clark Poetry Prize, and "Water Becomes Bone" (New Issues Press). He lives on a cottage farm in Southeastern Minnesota with his wife, Elizabeth Oness, and various beasts. The founding editor of Sutton Hoo Press, a literary fine press (www.suttonhoopress.com), he is also a potter and a re-emergent alpinist hungrily exploring our diminishing natural world.

John Torgrimson: Served as a Peace Corps Volunteer in the Solomon Islands. John went on to serve as Hong Kong Director for OXFAM. He was owner and editor-in-chief of the *Fillmore County Journal* newspaper for twelve years, then served as Executive Director of Seed Savers near Decorah, Iowa, and Acting Director of Eagle Bluff Environmental Center near Lanesboro, Minnesota. This is his essays second essay for *Lost Lake Folk Opera*. He also participated in *Folk Opera's* "Rural Economic Development Roundtable" in the Winter 2015 issue.

Sean Lause: Professor of English at Rhodes State College and an English teacher at Lima Central Catholic High School in Lima, Ohio, his poems have appeared in *The Minnesota Review, Another Chicago Magazine, The Beloit Poetry Journal* and *Lost*

Lake Folk Opera. His poetry collections include "Bestiary of Souls" (Future Cycle Press, 2013), "Wakeful Fathers," and "Dreaming Sons" (Orchard Street Press, 2017), and "Separation Anxiety" (Taj Mahal Review, 2022).

Emilio Regina: A published playwright in Canada with Eldridge Publishers, Brooklyn Plays, Big Dog Plays and I.E. Clark, to name a few, Emilio Regina is a retired high school Drama/English teacher. He currently works as an English auxiliary instructor at The College of the Rockies. Emilio lives in Kimberly, British Columbia, plays multiple instruments and performs as front man for the blues band The Hollers.

Robert Love: Operates Confluence Timber Company in Columbia Falls, Montana, where he resides with his wife Inez. His debut collection, "Pathfinder" from Rocket Science Press, is due to launch in the fall of 2022.

Leslie D. Soule: A fantasy author, Leslie recently completed her "Fallenwood Chronicles," a four-book series. She holds an MA from National University and is a citizen journalist. She has two books of poetry, "My Mentor, Death," and "Falling Through the World," both available from Terror House.

D.E. Green: Doug just retired from decades in the English Department at Augsburg University. He has published articles on Shakespeare, general-interest essays, and poetry. His poem "Gratitude" won the 2018 Martin Lake Journal Bookend Prize; other work has appeared in Bright Light: Stories in the Night, poems and artwork from Southeast Minnesota; in the 2021 Red Wing Arts Poet Artist Collaboration; and in several issues of *Willows Wept Review*. You can also find his poems on the sidewalks of his hometown, Northfield, Minnesota. His first collection, "Jumping the Median" (Encircle Publications, October 2019). Doug likes to say that he has been an occasional poet for thirty-five years.

Larry Gavin: Larry Gavin is a poet from Faribault, Minnesota. He is the author of five books of poetry.

Heather Candels: a former English teacher in Connecticut, now lives in Northfield, Minnesota. Her work has appeared in *The Prairie Home Companion Newsletter, Inkwell, The Widows Handbook: Poetic Reflections on Grief and Survival, Roux, Heart Lodge, Third Wednesday, The Lowdown, Xanadu, The Rockhurst Review*, and *Willows Wept Review*. She was also featured in No Small Measure, a broadside project pairing artists and poets funded by the University of North Georgia.

Rob Hardy: Northfield, Minnesota, Poet Laureate, Rob Hardy is the author of "Shelter in Place" (Finishing Line Press 2022), "Domestication: Collected Poems, 1996-2016" (Shipwreckt Books 2017), "The Collecting Jar" (Grayson Books 2005), and "Aeschylus, The Oresteia: An Adaptation" (Hero Now Theatre 2017). Rob's poetry and prose has appeared in *New England Review, Ploughshares, Rattle, New Letters, North Dakota Quarterly*, and other literary and scholarly journals. His adaptation of Aeschylus's *Oresteia* has been staged at Carleton College and by Hero Now Theatre in Minneapolis. Rob is former member of the Northfield School Board (2012-2020) and a Research Associate in Classics at Carleton College. He is and editor of "Bede, Historia Ecclesiastica Selections," and "Homer, Odyssey 9-12" (Dickinson College Commentaries).

Julie A. Ryan: Essayist, novelist, poet, and artist Julie's essays have been published in *Lost Lake Folk Opera*, as well as newspapers, and blogs. Her fiction has appeared in *The Clothesline Review*. Her socially relevant "When Life Was Still" trilogy was released in 2020. Julie's collection of concrete poems, "Relative Space," was published in 2021. Her poetry has also appeared in: *Writers' Night-A Sense of Place*, 2017; *Northfield Sidewalk Poetry*, 2018; *End in Mind Pandemic Poetry*, 2020.

Becky Boling: the Stephen R. Lewis, Jr. Professor of Spanish and the Liberal Arts at Carleton College, Emerita, she has published scholarly articles as well as poetry in the *Martin Lake Journal, Willow Wept Review*, and *Persimmon Tree*. Her poetry and prose appear online at *The Ekphrastic Review, visualverse.org*, and in several Writers' Night collections at the Northfield Public Library. Her short story, "Cassandra en su torre de papel," can be found online in *Proyecto Sherezade*. She is a winner in the Northfield Sidewalk Poetry Contest. Her poem, "shores," was featured in the Red Wing Arts XIX Poet Artist Collaboration. One of her poems was incorporated in the crowdsource community poem Kwame Alexander created and posted on NPR for Poetry Month, April 1, 2020. Becky was raised in southern Indiana, and she shivers in the colder but more welcoming state of Minnesota where she has raised a son and badly tended a garden.

Steve McGown: Steve McCown, a retired high school and parttime college teacher, graduated with a BA in English from Winona State University and an MA in English from Northern Arizona University. After teaching in the deserts of Southern California and Arizona for over thirty years, Steve returned to his native Minnesota, to Northfield, where he now resides with his wife Barbara and two semi-content cats. He is the author of "Ghosting" Up On Big Rock Poetry Series 2019).

Louis Martinelli: Louis Martinelli, poet, playwright, essayist, and educator, is a graduate of St. Mary's University and The University of Cincinnati. He was a Writer in Residence in many Midwestern communities and organizations, including The Mayo Clinic and the Northfield Arts Guild. His play, "Take My Hand," won a National Endowment for The Arts outstanding achievement award. Louis is literary executor of environmental writer Paul Gruchow's estate as well as founder and director of The Paul Gruchow Foundation.

Paul Gruchow: The author of many environmental books, he was once lauded as a contemporary Thoreau. Paul is also author of "Letters to a Young Madman." Sadly, Paul took his own life in 2004.

Tom Driscoll: Army veteran, returned Peace Corps Volunteer and program officer for the United States Agency for International Development, Tom Driscoll is author of many works of fiction, poetry and journalism, including literary journals, "Bleu: Selected Poems 1967–1997," and "Ondine & the Blue Troll—Ten Parables." Tom is the Managing editor and CEO of Shipwreckt Books Publishing Company & *Lost Lake Folk Opera* magazine.

$12.99

Lost Lake

Folk Opera

Vol 6
September 2020

Covid-19 2020
Special Issue& More

Back issues available on Amazon.